The Things I Love

The
Things
I
Love

Edited by Tony Palmer

Grosset & Dunlap
A FILMWAYS COMPANY
Publishers • New York

I dedicate this book to all of you who believe in the true meaning of love; love that is shared and not possessed, but cared for like a precious treasure that cannot be replaced.

Liberace

Contents

I Would Like To Be Remembered

as a kind and gentle soul, and as someone who made the world a little better place to live in because I had lived in it. Obviously, I would like to think that my music will be remembered. But I hope also that some of the beautiful things I have collected in my homes will be preserved. In fact, I have formed a trust so that my personal belongings and my homes will be shared by the world long after I have gone.

All of us are only here for a short time—I often feel that I am living on borrowed time. I should have been dead several years ago. But, fortunately, a greater power saw fit to spare me and give me this extra time to live. So every day is a truly marvellous gift to be enjoyed not just by me but by all the people who surround me. And one of

the best ways to repay all those who have given so generously to me, is for me to give to them.

I feel that all these beautiful things I live with have been placed in my care to look after. They don't really belong to me; they belong to the world. After all, they belonged to famous people before me—somewhere, somehow, they had been abandoned or not cared for. Then I came along and saw a broken chair or an unwanted dog or a forgotten antique that cried out to be saved.

I think it's my love of history that makes me want to restore

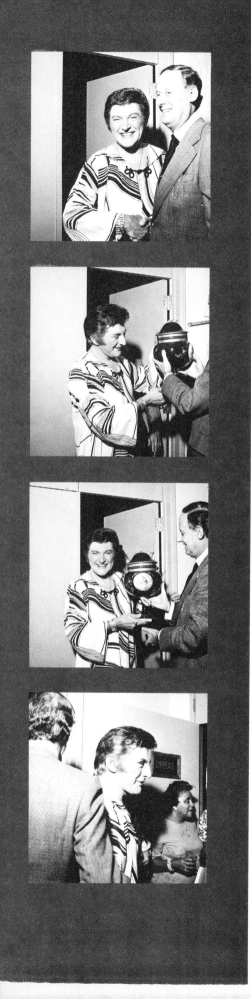

things. I find there is a great tendency, especially in our country, to tear out the old and build up the new—with no regard for tradition or the relics of the past. We have in America so *little* American history, except what we read in books, that often when we come across something truly old we merely take a picture of it and then put it in the annals of the public library. The thing itself is destroyed. It just makes me want to cry out "Save it!"

Once, when I was in Knoxville, Tennessee, I visited an old railroad station that was going to be torn down. I had heard they were selling some beautiful Tiffany glass windows for only $100 a piece, which was an absurdly low price. The only requirement was that, if you bought a Tiffany window, you had to replace it with plain glass so that the building itself would not suffer from the elements—in spite of the fact that eventually they were going to pull the whole place down anyway.

But while I was looking around, I discovered that this was the same railroad station used frequently by Abraham Lincoln. And yet they were going to wreck it and build another Freeway. So next day, when the editor of the Knoxville newspaper called me—he had heard I had visited the site—I told him how appalling it was to uproot this historical landmark. Consequently (and to my delight) he wrote an editorial based on my comments, proclaiming the railroad station an historical site and demanding that the new Freeway be moved to a location nearby.

So you can see that when I make up my mind, when I *really* make up my mind, my Taurus personality beams right through! I am total Taurus. And if you are born under the sign of Taurus, you are supposed to be strong, good at music and like expensive gifts! But, seriously, the world is full of places like that railroad station— I come across them constantly—and in a very small way I have been able to save a few of them. My homes, for instance, are all structures that would have been torn down had I not been able to save them . . . .

I can't tell you what happiness it gives me to find something I like, such as this urn on the left. I never collect merely to collect. Each item gives me a particular thrill, especially if it's been ignored or overlooked.

But collecting has its responsibilities. It's no good buying things and then not looking after them. My miniature pianos, for instance, are a nightmare to keep clean; but they are worth every last drop of effort, I'm sure you'll agree.

Greetings

By proclamation of the Mayor of

Knoxville, Tennessee, U. S. A.

Lee Liberace,

is hereby installed as an

Honorary Citizen

of the City of Knoxville
and is made a member of the Mayor's Staff

1792

Joh J. Duncan
Mayor of Knoxville

My efforts in restoring America's treasures occasionally receive official recognition, as you can see.

Anyone Can Build A House

if they have money. But to take something that is going to be destroyed and is dying, and make it live again—that is a very special thrill for me.

When I'm constructing one of my new houses, therefore, I supervise everything—from the carpeting up to the ceiling. I've discovered that a lot of people who build new houses lose interest when the actual building is completed. The interior design just doesn't interest them. But that's when I take over. I've been in a lot of homes that are beautifully built but are just sterile inside. They need those little touches: it needs some of those "Happy Happies," as I call them. The things that make people smile. The other day, for example, I went out and bought a leaded glass sign to put on the bar. All it says is "Bar." But it's a glowing, fun decoration. And these are the things that make people say: "Isn't that cute!" So they warm up a house, I always think.

And pictures. I try to buy pictures that are either colorful or amusing. And if I can't afford a Michelangelo, that is if I can't afford

the real thing, I'd rather have something that's been done by a young artist and that's . . . amusing. After all, when you talk about classic art, you are talking about millions and millions of dollars. And anyway, you never really own a masterpiece. It's been put in your trust for the time that . . . let's say for the time that you and your family survive. But you never really own it. I feel exactly the same about many of the authentic pieces of furniture in my home, all of them placed in my care to enjoy while I'm alive.

My problem is that I never throw anything away. That's why you will sometimes find an inexpensive piece right next to a very rare antique—because I cannot quite face discarding anything. I still have

a piece of furniture from my first home which was actually a one room apartment in New York. It's a cabinet—in fact, a small black and gold chest—and now sits in my Hollywood house. In New York I had just this one room, but I tried to fix it up as elegantly as I could because I believe you should always make the best of your surroundings, even when you don't have too much money.

I discovered my first dream palace in Hollywood, only a couple of minutes from Sunset Boulevard. It was not my first home in Los Angeles, as you will see, but it was the first which seized my imagination. Now, it's full of some of my most treasured possessions and one day I hope to be able to open it as a museum so that everyone can share with me the beautiful treasures and furniture and pianos I have collected. The proceeds from this museum will go into a foundation to support and promote new and undiscovered talent in the creative and performing arts.

Sunset Boulevard, of course, is one of the main thoroughfares of Hollywood. Yet my home has amazing privacy. It was originally built by Rudy Vallee, but was never lived in by him. It was one of fourteen estates in the Hollywood Hills constructed in the early twenties called Hacienda Acres. Most of them have been destroyed now, with the exception of this one which I was able to save. It too was ready to be torn down—no-one could afford the upkeep. It required too much maintenance. We are actually looking at the back end of the house. It's very difficult to photograph the front of the house because of a steep hill. It's only been photographed once from the front as far as I know and that was from a helicopter.

Everyone who visits me is constantly amazed that we have outdoor carpeting everywhere. We have green turf carpeting, which makes a perfect outdoor garden for entertaining. I have given some wonderful parties out here. After the sun goes down it's inclined to get a bit chilly, so we have outdoor heaters to heat the atmosphere. They're hidden in the trees so they're not noticeable. I can actually warm this entire outdoor area to about seventy degrees.

The main living room of my Hollywood house is dominated by a Baccarat crystal chandelier. It's unique because it combines many different elements. I found it originally in an antique shop. It had been tossed away in a corner. It was completely black, partly because it had had a gas burner installed in it. The shop owner was trying to show me all the gold candelabras, but I became intrigued by this

This is the grand staircase of my Hollywood house. The chandelier, which you see as soon as you come in the front door, sets the tone for the whole house. When I used to live here, I made many a good entrance down these stairs, I can tell you.

The back of the house, next to the pool. Luckily, you can't see the heaters I had installed in the trees and bushes to warm the temperature during parties. Nor can you detect the artificial carpeting, but that's because it's so good.

particular chandelier. And, as I was scratching it, I discovered that underneath its blackness was either brass or gold. So I bought it—very inexpensively—and had it cleaned up only to discover that it was really gold plated. Then I had it electrified and bought some Baccarat crystals in London to replace the gas burner. But I couldn't think how or where to hang it properly. I remembered a design I had seen in Versailles, so I set about copying it. First, I bought a beautiful picture frame and put it on the ceiling, replacing the picture with a mirror, and then suspended the chandelier from the center of the frame. (The mirror was, in fact, Victorian.) Finally, I added some cherubs around the side—they were French—and the result now adorns my living room. I think you'll agree, it looks magnificent!

Most of the gilt furniture in the house comes from an estate in Cincinnati. The chairs, however, were in a deplorable state when I found them, but I have had them restored and re-upholstered.

These two are particularly interesting. For many years they were used as studio rentals for movies. But they got too old and couldn't be used anymore. The upholstery, for example, had become completely threadbare. I had them re-covered with part of a tapestry I bought in Spain, and now they look as good as new.

As for the gold-leafing, I was lucky because I found an exceptional artist at recreating in marble and gold. He converted a blackened iron statue that was in my bedroom at Harold Way and transformed it into marble and gold. He also gold-leafed my front door so that it now looks like a solid hunk of gold. Apparently he covers the gold leaf with many layers of verathane, which is a transparent plastic that seals the gold and covers it just like glass.

With gold so expensive now, I'm sure glad I had most of my gold-leafing done years ago. It costs a fortune to use real gold leaf nowadays, and everything in my house at Harold Way is real gold. But then, the furniture calls for it. That style of furniture—most of it dates back to Napoleon and Louis XV—was always gilt. *Everything* was gilt.

The organ in the living room at Harold Way came with the house, so to speak. It was a fully blown pipe organ with an attachment that enabled you to play organ rolls, so it worked mechanically as well as manually. Quite unique, I'm told. There was an era back in the early twenties when every mansion had an organ in it. It was a status symbol. And this particular house, which was erected around 1925, was one of those mansions. Even so, at first it was not something I was greatly interested in—it was just too Boris Karloff for me.

The thing just turned me off from the start. Anyway, it didn't work. The house had been empty for so many years that the mice and the rats had gotten to the mechanism and chewed the bellows. It was so badly in need of repair that I tried to have it removed. Alas, nobody wanted it. Instead, everyone wanted *me* to fix it, or at least pay for its transportation. I just could not give it away.

So I decided that as long as I would have to spend money on getting rid of it, I might just as well spend money restoring it. So I moved it to a new location—where it no longer dominated the whole of the living room—had it gold-leafed and re-upholstered, and then rebuilt all its mechanics. To my surprise and delight I then discovered it contained all manner of novelty devices. For example, it possessed a great number of different musical instruments—xylophones, drums, cymbals, and even bird calls—all played from the keyboard. I must say that I have had a lot of fun with it.

The carpeting in the house was measured and designed by me and then I had it manufactured in Japan. The Japanese made it all by hand—it took them four and a half months. And the amazing thing about it was that when it arrived I had only about two inches of waste. I had measured it exactly right!

The onyx table has a curious history. Its base, not surprisingly, came first. In fact, it was originally sections of an altarpiece that came from Germany. I had bought these four separate pieces thinking they would make good legs for a coffee table. I had all the paint removed down to the old, original wood, and then coated them in gold leaf. Later I decided to use the pieces as legs for a table, so I had a frame built and began to look around for something which would make a stunning table top. Glass was too ordinary; so was marble. Somebody suggested onyx, because it would reflect all the colors of the room. So I sent a friend to Mexico to have a piece of onyx cut, and pretty soon I was in possession of the largest piece of cut onyx in existence. The original altar pieces had only cost about $200; but by the time I had the table made and the legs gold-leafed, the price was up to about $3,800. And that was before I had paid for the onyx!

But the most unusual table in this room dates from 1850 and was made for an Indian Maharajah by Baccarat in Paris. The entire table is Baccarat crystal. I bought it at a San Francisco antique fair where it was the *pièce de résistance* of the show and was not really for sale. It had been put on display as a glamorous lead item, to get

Above is the main sitting room in my Hollywood house, dominated by my Baccarat crystal chandelier, a triumph of restoration! You'd never believe how black and grimy it looked when I first saw it. And how tatty! Likewise the tapestry chairs on the right, not to mention the onyx table above. It's not the amount of money you spend, but what you spend it on.

Far left is my fabulous Baccarat crystal table, made for an Indian Maharajah. Bottom left, an armoire. And near left, just bits and pieces on a table I designed myself. Right, some Capo di Monte urns from Italy. Below is the bar which began life as a lean-to. Overleaf is the view from the bed in my master bedroom.

Above, the organ. I just couldn't give it away, so I had it restored

Right, the master bed with its llama bedspread. Again, when you consider all the different elements which went into making the bed the way it is, you will see it's not the amount you spend, but how you spend it. Below is a corner of my sitting room. You can just see Paderewski in the picture on the left.

The extension which got out of hand! Note the player-piano on the left, with the slot for piano-rolls above the keyboard.

Opposite, part of my Tom Mix dinner service. I think
I've lost count how many dinner services I have, but
this is a particular favorite, as is my set of silver
goblets, below. The gold table above was just a
mad extravagance, although I always think it adds a
certain something!

My sitting room. I've had some wonderful parties in here. You can see quite clearly the mirror on the ceiling from which I've suspended the chandelier. My Chopin piano is in the distance and the organ in the alcove on the right.

people into the show. Anyway, I told the organizers about my plans for a museum and that I couldn't think of a more appropriate place for it to go than in my home. Eventually, they decided to sell it to me. I understand there were only two of them ever made—one stayed in India, but the other somehow escaped!

This table was not a table originally. It was a "planter" from a graveyard—people used to put plants on top of it. But it seemed to me that such planters had other uses so I bought up as many as I could find and put glass tops on them, transforming them into coffee tables. I don't tell too many people, however, because they might get a little morbid. In fact, the windows in the antique shop I used to own were bevelled glass that came from a hearse. But they were very decorative and everyone wanted to buy them. I don't think they would have been quite so keen had they known where they had come from.

And this table I designed myself. I found some woodcarved candlesticks in a church and had them cut in half so that it appeared as if they came right through the glass top. I use this particular table to keep odd bits and pieces; I have some very old American cut glass, for example, that I have made into a lamp.

I have to admit that I possess a fabulous collection of crystal—all of it signed, either by the company which created it or by the individual artist.

So you can see that I have a predilection for turning something apparently useless into something of considerable use. Either something that would have been thrown away as being of no further value, or else something whose true potential had never been realized. I love changing things and giving them new life. I love *using* antiques, so that they don't just decay as museum pieces. These cabinets, for example, are French *armoires* which I have turned into silver cabinets merely by putting a light in the top, glass shelves, and a mirror at the back. (*Armoires* were used as closets or wardrobes in nineteenth century Europe—most of the old European homes didn't have closets, so they had these huge cabinets in which to hang clothes.) Once, I bought a whole collection of *armoires* before anybody knew what *armoires* were. Ten years ago you could buy each of them for $200 to $300. Now they are worth several thousand; so besides being a work of salvation, they also proved to be an excellent investment.

Anyway, I love the fake. As long as it *looks* real, I'll go for it. I discovered, for instance, that there is a process which takes an ordi-

nary metal object like a door knob and puts on a bronze finish to make it look very old. Apparently this is an old Chinese art, used by the Chinese many centuries ago. Usually there is a great emphasis on having the real thing as against the fake. I agree with that up to a point. But the movie studios, for example, were great at achieving the *look* of marble by painting it, or making a plain plaster wall look like wood panelling just by painting it. This, of course, is a great skill, just as it was in France during the time of Napoleon. Indeed, in Napoleon's time, the artificially created marble or woodwork was considered much more valuable than the real thing. There was an overabundance of marble used in monuments, homes, palaces, everywhere. When I stayed in Paris, for instance, in the Napoleonic suite at the Ritz, I noticed that some of the marble work there was "painted" marble and was over two hundred years old. And it has always been like that; I asked Mr. Ritz.

And speaking of Napoleon, these urns are French Sèvres. I would say they are about the most valuable pieces in the whole house.

My blue bar has an interesting story attached to it. Many people used to come out here just to look at the view; it is one of the best views of Hollywood you can get. But the nights in Hollywood are invariably cool. When we used to come outside to where the bar now is and look at the view, everyone would start shivering. I had a few parties out here where I tried putting braziers to warm up the terrace. But it remained too chilly or too damp. So I thought, "Wouldn't it be nice, since this is such a marvellous view of Hollywood, to have a room out here with a roof that you could heat." A little anteroom, added onto the living room. Typically, it got more involved than that.

First, I decided to screen off the porch with glass. But I forgot to allow for the height of the living room being different from the height of the back of the house, so I had to devise this dome to compensate for the differences in levels! Then I had to build a bar; then I had to tile the floor . . . and so on. But once again it gave me the excuse to build something out of nothing. The tiles are from Italy, for example. I had bought them long before I ever had a use for them. They were just so beautiful that I had thought, "Somewhere, some day, some place, I am going to have a room with these tiles." This "porch" gave me the answer. In fact, the tiles helped me decide the coloring of the whole room—turquoise. The tables are iron, but I had them painted in turquoise as well. The fireplace is also iron.

I am most proud, however, of these candelabras. They come from the Dream Prince, Ludwig of Bavaria, and contain the largest piece

of opaline glass that has ever been discovered. Every one of these candleholders is numbered and they are all handmade.

My blue room also includes a lot of glass, from Murano in Venice. When I first went through their factory, I was so impressed with what I saw that I wanted *everything!* Eventually, I came across some marvellous brandy snifters with an N engraved on the side. I said, "Oh, my God, I have *got* to have some of those. Could you engrave an L on each piece, please?" But the manager said, "Well, why do you want L's?" I said, "Because my name is Liberace." He said, "But you don't understand, sir. They are Napoleon brandies. You serve Napoleon brandy in it. They *always* have an N on them, surrounded by a wreath of ivy." But I said, "Put an L on them." So he put an L, and I now have the only Napoleon brandy glasses with L's instead of N's.

This is my bedroom. How do you like it? It's French Victorian and most of the furnishings are antiques. The cabinets are French Boule designed by André Boule early in the 18th century. The bed, however, is made up from old carvings done by Spanish artisans that I discovered right here in Los Angeles. And the bed-end was actually a cornice over a door, from a library in Spain. The bedspread is made of llama and ermine tails. When my business manager got the bill, he called me up—very irate—and said, "You've gone too far. Sixty-five hundred for a bedspread!" And just that day in the paper I had read that Herb Alpert had spent $165,000 for a bedspread made out of chinchilla. So I said, "You don't know how lucky you are. Herb Alpert has just spent $165,000; *this* is just a drop in the bucket." Anyway the bed is really a marvellous creation out of nothing, nothing but bits and pieces.

After a while, you know, one becomes an incurable collector. You just collect to collect. I have an entire dinner service, for example, that belonged to Tom Mix, the famous Western movie star. All of the pieces are monogrammed with an M. I have had offers to sell it at tremendous profit to people who have the same initials, but I refused because there was only one Tom Mix and his dinner service represents an era when Hollywood was the glamour capital of the world.

Even so, I have never become that attached to what I collect. I

Everywhere you look, there's a mirror. I always think they add so much depth and richness to a room—as long as they're surrounded by gilt, that is!

Left, my screening room. I love showing old movies—I have quite a collection. Below, two of the horses I found in a shop in Liverpool; they seem to be almost leaping off the page.

Looking along the blue bar—that extension again! The fireplace in the center is false, although it looks real enough. When you're seated at the bar in one of these chairs, you can see for miles along Sunset Boulevard. It's very spectacular.

am fond of *some* things, of course, but unless I come across a treasure or something that is truly one of a kind, I find myself giving away a lot of things. In fact, in the last few years, instead of going Christmas shopping, I just go through my homes and select presents—because I have better things in my home than I can find in the stores! Anyway, the things that I *know* will make people happy, I couldn't possibly miss. I just say, "Well, I know so-and-so was here one day and he admired this or she admired that so I will wrap it up." I know that I'm far from broke, but my friends sometimes say I'm much too generous. But I don't *enjoy* life unless I can give to somebody here or somebody there. Admittedly, my antiques are an excellent investment. But that is not the reason I buy them. If it were, I would never give any of them away.

But being a collector, especially if you are not a professional, can be full of dangers. Sometimes you think you have a bargain and all you have is a piece of junk. So you have to take chances. Much of my silver I acquired in Liverpool, England, from a marvellous place on Scotland Road, which I was led to by the wife of the American ambassador. She said, "You must go to this place. It is owned by a very eccentric old lady who has treasures that you can't believe. But, be warned. She is *very* eccentric."

So off we went. The first time I went there, I took my Cadillac limousine. The old lady would *not* let us in. She talked through the door. I told her who I was. Eventually she said, "Well, get rid of that big car and come back in a taxi." So we did, and then she let us in. And we fell in love with her, and she fell in love with us. The whole show company—I had about 16 people in my show at that time—made daily journeys to Scotland Road. There we would find these treasures that were comparatively inexpensive. And every night, after the show, we would have polishing parties. We would take the stuff home and go up to my suite to polish! Among the things we found was a painting for which she wanted $100. Later, it turned out to be a Sir Godfrey Neller, worth $25,000. So she did have some treasures!

I have often been lucky in my rummaging around, however. These horses, for instance, I found right here in Hollywood, in a little junk shop! They were painted white and were very dirty. But I took them home and soaked them in a soapy solution to get them clean. To my surprise, the paint started to peel off, and underneath the paint was sterling silver. So if you don't take chances while you're looking for antiques, you will never find that priceless bargain.

My house in Hollywood is full of a strange mixture of valuable antiques and junk, all of it chosen by me. But I don't think you measure the worth of an object by the amount you paid for it, any-more than you value the worth of a person by the number of dollars he or she has in the bank. The important consideration—both about collecting and about decorating a house—is to enjoy what you are doing, and to have around you those things that give you pleasure and, which you hope, thereby, will give other people pleasure. And to do that, you don't necessarily need piles of money.

Often, I find it fun to act like I don't have a single penny. Any-way, I *love* free things and bargains. I used to love buying canned chickens that were only 69 cents a can. Apart from the fact that the chicken was delicious, I had a quiet laugh knowing that everyone who complimented me so highly on the chicken was, in fact, eating canned chicken which only cost 69 cents. And when I find a bargain, I'll buy $200 worth of it! One time, I found a pair of shoes I liked. "What colors do they come in?" I asked. They said, "Black, brown, gray and green." I said, "OK. I'll take all four." It may sound extravagant, and probably it was. But the store owner was happy, I was happy, the people with me were happy, so what could have been wrong with it? It was certainly not half as crazy as some of my other clothing expedi-tions! But more about my costumes later.

Now you see on the left what I mean about that fireplace. I don't possess a great collection of pictures, but I particularly like this seascape. I always find the sea so eternally fascinating.

How It All Began

I realized very, very early in my career that the demands of being a concert pianist were not for me. I had always wanted to have fun with my work. I never wanted it to make me into something that I really didn't want to become. I was *happy* playing classical music. I loved it. But the people for whom I played the classical music were not the people I wanted to please.

Early in my career I had travelled as a concert pianist and had often played to a handful of musical purists. But I longed to please the man on the street, the people who had relatively little appreciation of music. I feel now that I have given these people a musical awareness that otherwise they might never have had. So I have no regrets. I still love classical music and, obviously, there is a place for the Rubinsteins and the Horowitzes. But, as a critic once wrote in a review of a concert I gave in San Francisco several years ago: "Liberace is no Rubinstein. But neither is Rubinstein a Liberace."

Me, aged 8, with my dog Queenie.

Often I am invited by symphony conductors to appear with their orchestras. Usually, however, they preface the invitation by saying, "I heard you play some Chopin and I was completely taken aback to find that you are as good a musician as you are." I take that as a compliment, of course, I know, in my heart of hearts, I am not the greatest pianist in the world. (Certainly, there are greater virtuosos than I am). But I have been able to do with the piano something that maybe even the greatest virtuosos have been unable to do. I have been able to reach the people. I have spoken in a musical language that has been understood by people of all nationalities.

I never underestimate the power of a smile or of a friendly handshake; I think people can look into your eyes and discover your true self without ever hearing a spoken word. But the greatest common denominator I have found in my life has been this musical language that I am privileged to speak. Sometimes our diplomats fail with the spoken word, whereas our musicians and our entertainers conquer. It's a marvellous thing, for instance, that today we are increasing our cultural exchanges with foreign countries. Someone interviewed me recently and asked how I would feel if I was invited to play in China. I said, "Well, if Ping-Pong players can get a message across, I think I could too."

I was born in West Allis, Wisconsin, which is a suburb of Milwaukee. I was the third child of an Italian father, who came from a fishing village near Naples called Formia. I began studying when I was four, and won a scholarship to the Wisconsin College of Music when I was seven and a half. That lasted for 17 years, which was the longest scholarship that had ever been awarded.

In fact, I came from a very musical family. My father was a French horn player, and my mother's family was also musical. They all played some kind of musical instrument; my mother's only sister was a Doctor of Music at St. Joseph's Convent and taught violin and piano and played the organ.

My brother George studied the violin and later taught at North Western Conservatory. He also played with various name bands during the big-band era. My sister was a professional pianist, and at 16 performed with the Milwaukee Symphony Orchestra. Later, she

Below, and left to right, that's me in the cap, Brother George holding my dog, my cousin Esther and my sister Angie. This was taken at the time I was attending the Wisconsin College of Music in the early thirties.

50

abandoned her promising musical career to go into medicine and became an X-ray technician.

We always had some form of music in the home, even though it was usually thought an extra. We had the only RCA orthophonic phonograph in the neighborhood; naturally it played records more beautifully than any other record player! But it was a tremendous luxury. I remember my mother and father having the most noisy argument over it. We needed many other things, my mother argued, but my father always spent his money on the phonogram because it reproduced the sound of music so beautifully. My father said it was more important to have music in the house than even food.

My mother was more practical. She worried about whether we had clothes, whether we had coal for the fire and food on the table. My dad was more aesthetic. He'd save up his money and take me to concerts which we could not really afford.

We lived in a very modest bungalow on the south side of Milwaukee, in a village called West Milwaukee. It was part of a new development. You didn't dare go home in the dark because you might walk in the wrong house—they all looked so much alike. But

Far left is my father, a distinguished French horn player. Above left, the house in which I was born, at West Allis, Wisconsin. Immediately above, on the left is my Uncle John and on the right is my Uncle Mike, both of whom played with my father.

my mother had a green thumb and was able to plant things and improve the landscaping. And we did have something that none of the other people had. We had a front porch. Screened in with storm windows for the winter, it made our house look just that little bit different. We could sit out there and feel mighty proud of our front porch.

The house had a downstairs kitchen and an upstairs kitchen. The downstairs kitchen was where all the cooking took place, and the upstairs kitchen was for company. We also had a living room into which we were hardly ever permitted to go, except that my sister and I were allowed in because that was where the piano was.

I used to practice a great deal. And because of my studies, I was going to Music College at the same time as I was going to High School. I was the only student at West Milwaukee High School who was allowed to arrive at school after 11:30 in the morning; the other kids had to be there at 8:15. But, because of my musical studies, I was given permission to be late.

We were brought up during the Depression years and these were very difficult times for my family. We had to manage somehow with our own natural resources. My mother worked in a cookie factory; my brother George worked in a sandwich shop; my sister did house-work on the side. I played anywhere and anyplace I could make a dollar. I never had to do any manual labor, however, although I worked once in a restaurant and washed dishes and waited on tables. In fact, I was a very bad waiter and an even worse dishwasher. I scalded both of my hands by washing dishes.

There was also a time when I was the sole supporter of the family. When my brother lost his job and my sister lost her job and my mother wasn't working, I was the only one in the family who was able to work. My school gave me special privileges so that I could work at night, go to Wisconsin College of Music in the morning, and then on to the High School by midday. In the evening, after dinner

Mother with two proud sons. George studied violin and played with many of the famous bands during the Swing Era. Right is my favorite portrait of my mother.

Me at various stages of growing up. Note the smile! George and Rudy are washing our car (not one of mine!); and on the right the Liberace brothers, in their gangster pose, from left, me, George, and Rudy.

Above, with a heavy group of musicians! Actually, it was an end of term concert at high school. On the right, an end of term play in which I portrayed Haile Selassie.

and a nap, I would go off to work again, and the whole routine would start all over. In fact, my first professional engagement was actually when I was still going to grade school. It was an engagement my father strongly objected to: he said it was unworthy of my talents. We used to have silent movies at school (because we couldn't afford the sound ones) and I got the job of accompanying the films with the piano. Admission for the movies was three cents in the afternoon for students and five cents in the evening for adults. I got 50 cents a week!

But, although we were poor, we always managed to have a good meal on the table. My mother and father were both very inventive about cooking. They could take inexpensive ingredients and make gourmet meals out of them. What the butcher used to throw away, we used to make meals out of. Kidneys, sweetbreads, tripe, things that were not usually found on the American dining table.

I was beginning, however, to think that my musical skills had no value, that what I had to offer had no worth. It seemed that I was destined to struggle for years, and for nothing; that I had been born into a period when everybody wanted entertainment, but they wanted it for free. I did benefit after benefit, and free show after free show. I began to wonder whether I would ever make a proper living out of what I was doing. Maybe I should learn some other trade, my father told me. For a while, I seriously thought that I should develop my talents in the kitchen. I could always be a chef or something, because even then I loved creating good food. The first real money I ever earned was a dollar a night, although, admittedly, in those days a dollar bought a lot of things.

During my scholarship term, however, I made my debut as a concert pianist with the Society of Musical Arts in Milwaukee. And

at 19, my first professional solo appearance was with the Chicago Symphony Orchestra. Only then did my father—who, after all, was himself a dedicated classical musician—finally relent. He told me, "Now you can go your own way and play any kind of music you want. You have proven to me that you are an artist, and that you are capable of being a true virtuoso. Now you are free to choose for yourself."

My concert with the Chicago Symphony Orchestra was an enormous challenge for me. I had done recitals and things like that many times before. In fact, I had started playing recitals when I was about 13 and by now took them as a matter of course. But playing with a major symphony orchestra was a whole different ball game. I felt a tremendous responsibility of co-ordinating with nearly a hundred other musicians.

But I have to confess that I was not nervous. I remember Dr. Frederick Stock (the conductor), who was in his late seventies, being more nervous than I was. He said to me, "How is it that you appear to be so calm?" I told him I would not dream of going out on the stage unless I was fully prepared. I think that was my whole secret. It seemed to me that if you appear in front of the public to make a speech or to perform an act or to make any kind of public display before an audience, it's only when you don't know what you are going to say or what you are going to play that you get nervous. Nervousness seems to me a form of insecurity. The people who are terribly nervous are usually those who are unsure about what they are going to do. For my very first concert with the Chicago Symphony Orchestra—in which I played the Liszt Concerto in A Major—I had rehearsed the piece so thoroughly that I could play it backwards, forwards and upside down. In fact, I had actually put the concerto aside a while before the concert because I was afraid of becoming stale. I can remember it now—the concerto was sixty-seven pages long. I had totally memorized it. Plus I had to remember all my entrances, where the orchestra played, when to come in, and when to stop. The concert was a great training. Even now, whenever I go out on the stage, I am extremely well prepared. If I break in a new number, I try to do it on the road at some smaller concert hall where, if I did happen to make a mistake, I wouldn't be too severely criticized. Only when I am fully satisfied with my performance will I introduce the new piece into my Las Vegas act, or some other place where I am going to be confronted with music critics.

Left, laying a wreath at the tomb of Paderewski. Above, night club life in the late thirties. It was fun, but not especially glamorous as you can see.

But although my debut with the Chicago Symphony Orchestra was all very grand and glorious, it didn't pay the rent. Even when I had started my career as a concert pianist, the performances that brought money home to the family were those I did aside from the classical things. I'm not putting down classical music, because it too can be lucrative. But at that time it wasn't. In fact, my father was out of work for seven years. Who needed a French horn player? Saxophone players or trumpet players could always work in a dance band, but my dad could not. So I played for dancing schools; I even had a little dance band of my own. Three or four piece, you know. And we played for road houses and private parties at weekends. I was able to make a living, just, and, in between times, carry on with my classical studies.

I also found that, in some of my early concertizing, I would ask the audience for requests and people would call out for Gershwin or Cole Porter. One day, someone shouted for "The Three Little Fishes." So, for a joke, instead of playing it straight, I began to play it in the various styles of different classical composers. It was a great success, and pretty soon I started getting offers to give performances in supper clubs. There, people were out for an evening's entertainment, and it was hard to hold their attention unless I added some dialogue or patter. Condensing the classics, however, in order to amuse these late-night audiences proved to be very popular. In my recitals, of course, people sat motionless for twenty-five minutes just to listen to one number. But they wouldn't do so in a night club. They would walk out.

I left Milwaukee in 1941 and went East to make my big splash. I was already twenty-one years old and figured I had gone as far as I could in my home town. I had the best jobs, the best work, and was the most sought-after pianist in town. Indeed, I had more work than I could handle, but I was still only a big frog in a little pond. I felt I wasn't getting the recognition I deserved.

My big desire was to go to New York. I thought that was the moon. Alas, I only got as far as New Jersey, partly because somebody told me I should take a job in New Jersey, since a lot of New Yorkers lived there and I would be discovered. Well, I wasn't. I played at a place called Pal's Tavern in West Orange, New Jersey, for about six months. But I kept going to New York and sitting on agents' doorsteps until finally I got someone interested enough in me to come over and listen. I'll never forget the occasion. They were impressed and

signed me up. I really thought I had arrived, especially since I had joined the biggest entertainment agency in America, MCA, the Music Corporation of America!

However, I soon discovered that I was actually at the *bottom* of the list. If anybody called in to hire an act, everyone else was mentioned first. When they got down to me they'd say, "Who's Liberace?" Nobody knew *who* I was. Once again, I was broke. Once again, I hired myself out to anyone who needed a piano player. There was a particular couple who engaged me through MCA to play at a party they were giving in upstate New York. The bus fare was around two dollars which was all the money I had. I played the evening and everyone loved me. My gracious hosts thanked me and casually mentioned that my fare back to New York would be paid by my agency, which was the customary procedure. How was I going to get back to New York? Hitchhike in a tuxedo? No, I was too proud to do that. I glanced at the bus schedule in my pocket until I was sure that the last bus had left, and then I went to my host and confirmed that I had missed the last bus because I was having such a wonderful time at their party. They graciously had me driven back to New York in their chauffered limousine. They were Mr. and Mrs. Paul Getty, and we became very good friends.

I realized, of course, that I would have to do something dramatic in order to make a name for myself. I would have to do *something* to take myself off the bottom of that list. So I went on a campaign, as it were, of self-publicity. I just bombarded people continuously with announcements of what I was doing. There used to be a time when you could send out what they called a penny post. So I used the penny postcard because it was the cheapest form of advertising I could think of. Everyone who ever gave me their calling card or their business card got on my list. Actually I had gotten the idea from Sophie Tucker. Every person she had ever met in her lifetime was put on her mailing list.

Before I knew it, I had a following! People said, "I got your card. Here it is!" In fact, it was a penny postcard that first brought me to Las Vegas in 1944. I had sent a card to the Entertainment Director of the Last Frontier Hotel (whom I had never met in my life) and, believe it or not, it was answered. I was appearing at the Mount Royal Hotel in Montreal, Canada, when, to my surprise, I got a call from a Miss Maxine Lewis who turned out to be the Entertainment Director of the Last Frontier. "Yes," she said. "I have heard of you. Would you be interested in playing Las Vegas?" I was amazed. I said I would love to play Las Vegas, but, I added cautiously, I make a lot of money. Then, shamelessly, I lied about my salary. I was actually making $350 a week at the Mount Royal Hotel, so just for the hell of it I doubled it. I told Miss Lewis I was getting $700 per week. She said, "Well, that will be just fine."

The opening show was one of the great thrills of my life. People in Las Vegas accepted me instantly, just like magic. Except that after a few days, Maxine called me into her office and said "I want to complain." I thought she didn't like me or something. But she said, "We're not paying you enough," and automatically doubled my salary. She gave me $1500 for my first engagement in Las Vegas! I just couldn't believe it. I had never made that kind of money in my life. To go up to four figures was the hardest thing imaginable. Anyway, having a taste of success and the money it brought, I could never go back. Whenever anybody now offered me a job in a place I had worked previously, I said, "Well, I would love to come back, but as you know I now get $1500 a week so, alas, I can't afford to."

64

Dad, with two proud sons. And below, Mom, watchful as ever.

Maxine was so marvellous to me. She told me that the next time I came back they would give me another raise. So the next time I went back, they gave me $2500 per week. In all, I played twenty-five engagements at the Last Frontier before I opened the Riviera Hotel in 1954. And by 1954 I was making $50,000 per week.

The mid-forties and immediately after the war was also the time in America of the supper clubs. Every major hotel in the country had a supper club—the Waldorf Astoria, the Palmer House in Chicago, the Persian Room at the Plaza in New York. They all had a supper and show room. And these made for a family kind of audience. If mom and dad came, they brought the kids. So I got to know the children. And as the children grew up, I got to know *their* children. Thus I have grown up with my audience just as my audience has grown up with me. I guess that is also true of Sinatra and Presley and a great number of entertainers who started out with, primarily, a teenage following, just as I did. When those teenagers grew up and had families of their own, the teenage audience became the family audience. It's certainly not true, therefore, that my audience is just silver-haired moms.

That image started more or less with the Press, I believe. Apparently it made a better picture if all the kids and all the men stepped aside and just left the ladies. It happened many times, and at the

time I never thought anything about it. But now I think it created the wrong impression, especially as the Press photographers always made even the younger ladies step away, leaving just the older ones. I remember some of the headlines: "Get Ready, Mom. He is Coming." It was all a bit misleading. And I suppose the fact that I introduced my mother on television and made her meet so many people induced a lot of other mothers to admire me. I don't think it would have worked quite so well had I pushed my father into the spotlight, for example. Anyway, by this time my father and mother had been divorced for some years. Mother was living with me and had become very much a part of my happiness.

I think my parents' divorce in fact brought our family much closer together. When my sister and my older brother got married, I had to make a home for myself that included my mother and my kid brother. They became my immediate family. My kid brother died, and my mother has lived alone for a number of years, but we have always remained very close.

Apart from the supper clubs, there were also many night clubs. When you speak of night clubs now, they all seem to be confined to the state of Nevada, in Reno or Las Vegas. But in the late forties every state had a group of major night clubs. Chicago had the Chez Paree, New York had the Copacabana, San Francisco had the Vene-

Las Vegas, here I come! Outside the Riviera, in the mid-fifties. And below —there was no escaping Mom's cooking. Little wonder I need three sizes of clothes.

tian Rooms. I hated playing these clubs at first because the audiences were so noisy. And there were no such things as microphones. They were used in radio, but never in night clubs. You had to have a natural delivery; your voice had to be pure, and you had to learn how to project your voice without mechanical devices. So I had to study vocal projection with a fine teacher in Chicago. "After all," she said. "Opera singers don't use microphones." You can whisper and still be heard, provided you project your voice and send it out on natural air waves. That's why the auditoriums of the past were so great, because they were built acoustically. You could literally hear a pin drop. So, all in all, night clubs helped me learn my craft even more thoroughly. And when I realized that the night club industry was fading away, I began to concentrate on playing theaters and concerts where people came specifically to see a show and not to have drinks or dinner.

I had always felt that you had a much better chance of doing your best if there were no distractions—drinking and eating, after all, *are* a distraction during a performance. The hotels in Las Vegas handle it beautifully. They try to get people served and fed *before* the show starts. But it's an impossibility. When I come on stage at the Hilton, I would say 90% of the audience is still eating. And it's hard to applaud with a fork in your hand! A lot of performers use the opening acts on their show while everyone finishes their dinner. I never do. So my opening is usually a good hunk of music that uses up ten or twelve minutes while everyone stops eating. I don't do too much dialogue in which the audience might have to laugh. Imagine laughing with a hunk of steak in your mouth!

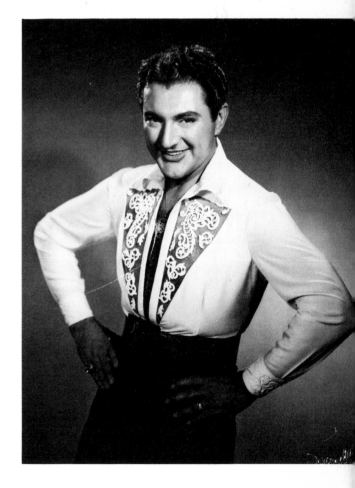

But there was another reason that took me away from the supper clubs. When I used to perform in the top clubs of America, I would receive a standing ovation at, say, the Waldorf Astoria, playing some light classics. But then, having changed my clothes, I would walk out afterward on to the street and become a complete nonentity. Nobody on the street knew who I was, and this bothered me. I think that one of the great accomplishments in my life, therefore, is that I am now the most recognized person, the most waved at person—let's put it this way: from taxi drivers to truck drivers, from waitresses and waiters to the ladies who are polishing the floor in the lobby of the hotel—they all look up as they recognize me. They know me. They feel they know my family also and, invariably, they greet me with "How's your mother?" or "How is George?" And I love it. I think I would have been very, very lonely had I remained a concert pianist.

My Piano-shaped World

The idea of having everything piano-shaped began, curiously enough, as a publicity gimmick. As far as I remember, the very first piano-shaped thing of all was the swimming pool at my house in the Valley. It was the best way I could think of, of getting a pool free. I said to the supplier, "If you make this pool for me, it will get a lot of publicity. So it had better not cost me anything." And it didn't. Then I discovered that if I offered to have my light fixtures molded into the shape of a piano, I would get *those* free as well. Eventually, the only thing in the house on which I spent my money were the bricks and mortar. Almost everything else was given me, including the furniture.

But, as I discovered to my cost, in other ways it was a considerable price to pay—I had sold my privacy. I stupidly mentioned the house on television and said to the watching millions, "If you are ever in California, drop by." Alas, they didn't just drop by; they dropped in. By the thousand. The house happened to be on a corner, and so was unprotected by any fence to keep the people back. Do you know that before long we were not able to open our curtains in the dining room or the living room because if and when we did, people came and

pressed their noses up against the glass. So we had to keep the curtains closed. And the doorbell just kept ringing all the time. Soon we were like a public exhibition, second only to Disneyland. Even in the backyard, where I was allowed a six-foot fence because of the swimming pool, I had no real protection. I used to wake up sometimes in the morning and find that people had scaled the fence and were taking pictures and sitting on the lawn furniture as if they had a perfect right to do so.

I suppose I had asked for it. And I know I learned my lesson. Now, in Palm Springs, although I have a home that is right in the center of town, it is completely protected. I'm always pleased to have people drive by and take a look, but from the outside. Behind my fence, I have all the privacy I need; that is, until I go out. Then, at least, I am prepared. When you go out in public, you have to expect to *meet* the public, and they have a right to meet you. But when you are in the confines of your home and gardens, you should have an equal right: privacy.

But it took me a long time to learn that particular lesson. Possibly the most daring thing I ever did was during one Christmas. In the Valley, there was a tradition that everyone decorated the outside of their homes. Very lavishly. As I had been made Honorary Mayor of Sherman Oaks, I was expected to go further than anybody else. And naturally, being me, I went in for some truly spectacular Christmas decorations. Indeed, the decorations were so extraordinary, that during the Christmas holidays the police had to direct the traffic that jammed up in front of my home. Almost eight thousand cars passed by every night, simply to look at the Christmas decorations. We had music playing and the sound of my voice booming out over loudspeakers. I used to talk to the people from inside the house, wishing them happy holidays and a Merry Christmas. The house became a real tourist attraction.

But in fact it was like living in a fish bowl. I couldn't even get into my garage. We had to look out of the windows to see if the coast was clear! Ninety-nine percent of the people who came by enjoyed it, and shared it and loved it. The other one percent, alas, caused us a lot of grief. There were a few people who were jealous, or who perhaps didn't like me. They broke windows and threw eggs at the front door. Only a handful, but it was enough to sour the whole effort. Eventually we had to put a twenty-four hour guard on the house to ensure our safety. And it was the idea that my home was

Left, my piano-shaped pool. It began almost as a joke, but pretty soon the joke got out of hand. Would you believe that people used to scale that fence and sit beside the pool as if it were their own. Overleaf, left, is my André Boulle piano from France, it was a gift from Mrs. Thelma Kieckhefer of Phoenix, Arizona. Right, above, some of my miniatures. On the top right, if you take a close look, is the pornographic piano. Bottom right is my piano-shaped desk. The keys, I'm afraid, are false.

Above, more of my
miniature pianos; I have
over a thousand. Top
right, you can see models
of Mom, George and me.
Cute, don't you think? At
the right is a crazy piano
that my friends and I
decorated ourselves during
a party. Just take a tube of
glue, I said, a few
sparklers, and do your
thing. I use it for my
honky-tonk routine.

Above, one of my most precious miniatures, all jewelled. Right, an original player-piano. And below, the piano on which I used to practice.

*My Chopin piano. I've had this restored to its
original condition, which is just as well considering
Paderewski is keeping a watchful eye!*

only safe if protected by an armed guard which finally decided me to sell it and move on. Maybe the piano-shaped gimmick had not been such a good idea after all.

I got my first real piano, however, when I was at my lowest financial ebb. I was staying at a household in Hollywood where I was referred to as "The man who came to dinner." I had just come to dinner one night but had stayed a year. I had first met my host—he was called Clarence Goodwin—in Boston, while he was attending a convention. He had given me his business card (he worked in the shoe trade) and said, "If you are ever out in California, look us up." So I did. I looked them up and went for dinner. Late that evening they asked me if I had anywhere permanent to stay and I said I had not. "Well," they said. "We happen to have a spare room so why not move in with us?" They had fallen in love with me and I with them. Pretty soon I became part of their household, and we have remained dear friends to this day.

Mr. Goodwin also took it upon himself to act as my business manager. So whenever I got any offers, he was able to raise my salary by telling everyone about all the offers that I was having to turn down. Since I had a nice home in which I could stay for as long as I wished, I had all the financial and social security I needed for the present. Consequently, as far as my career was concerned, Mr. Goodwin was going to make quite sure I gave the impression of being very hard to get.

I think my pianos often get better treatment on the road than I do. When I'm on tour, I have three on the move, leapfrogging engagements, if you see what I mean, just to make sure I always have my instrument at the right place at the right time.

About this time I came across a beautiful Blüthner concert grand piano in one of the music stores of Hollywood. It was ten feet long and utterly magnificent. I had never seen a piano like it. It had four strings to each note, for example, instead of the conventional three. Apparently, it was the last one like it to get out of Germany before the war. During the war, alas, the Blüthner factory had been bombed, so now there were only two of these pianos remaining. I discovered later that the one which had remained in Europe had also been destroyed. Consequently, this was now the only one of its kind. But there was no way I could afford such a superb instrument, so I came back to the Goodwin's house extremely depressed. I told Mr. Goodwin I had played on a piano that was very like taking a trip to heaven. I must have seemed elated because Mr. Goodwin said that clearly I should have that piano. Alas, I said, I should have a lot of things but I can't afford them.

Just a little practice piano.
On the right is my latest protégé,
Vince Cardell.

The next day that piano was in their living room. He had bought it. And he made arrangements for me to pay him back a little at a time as I was working. What could I say? I was overwhelmed by Mr. Goodwin's kindness. But it turned out to be a shrewd investment. With my new piano, Mr. Goodwin managed to get even bigger increases in my salary! I was able to pay him back in less than a year. And I still have that piano today.

My miniature piano collection started when I was a child. I think I was about seven when I acquired my first piece. Now I have over one thousand, although some are duplicates. But the first is the one I treasure most. It was actually given me by the great Polish pianist, Paderewski. It was a replica, he told me, of a piano he had played on in Budapest. It is a small, silver piano which he sent me through my family as a memento of when I had played for him. Whenever anyone came over to the house, I would haul out this little piano as my greatest treasure and proudly display it to all my friends.

Through the years, of course, as people have realized that I collect miniatures, I have been sent tiny pianos made out of every kind of material imaginable. Some have only sentimental value, but some are genuine antiques. I have one given me by a Mrs. Lawrence Fisher from Detroit, Michigan, that is worth upwards of $25,000. A little bird comes out and sings whenever you press a button.

I also have an early nineteenth-century French pornographic piano, which I am told is quite unusual. In those days, pornography was considered an art—everyone collected pornography. It is hand painted on porcelain and looks perfectly innocent on the outside. But on the inside . . .

I have several miniatures given me by celebrities I have worked with, many of them autographed. I have pianos that are made of marble, some of glass, and others of wood. I have some made out of ceramic and molded to look like me and my family. And I even have one little piano inside which there are tape recordings that play some of my music. It is just *adorable*. It is covered in antique white and gold leaf, and dotted with little rhinestones. It looks exactly like the piano I use on stage when I do my rinky-dink routine.

But I also have a collection of larger pianos. I had always been taught from childhood that a musician is only as good as his instrument. I used to look forward to taking my piano lessons, for example, because my teacher's apartment housed a really fine piano. Most of my practicing I did at college, which possessed several excellent

pianos. Alas, they were so much more satisfying than playing on the upright piano at home, which was a little tired and worn.

Anyway, after my lucky Blüthner, I began to acquire pianos like other people acquire potted plants. I was helped by a friend who happened to be a piano dealer. He was in the business, and still is. He buys and sells pianos and rents his more spectacular instruments to the movie studios. Consequently, he is always on the look out for rare and beautiful instruments. Sometimes just for photographic purposes. And whenever he discovers a really super piano, he lets me know.

My latest acquisition—which I came across thanks to an antique-dealer friend—is a Pleyel from Paris. This is a piano that Chopin played on. It is all hand painted and its hand carved case is truly magnificent. It is in excellent playing condition.

One day my friend rang to say that he had a new and very unusual piano for me to look at. "And I don't think you have ever seen one like it," he added. It turned out to be an experimental piano with two keyboards. Someone had designed an instrument to enable a single player to play two pianos at the same time. At least, that's what it seemed.

Another piano is part of my André Boulle collection that I started several years ago; in fact, the piano was donated by a Mrs. Kieckhefer of Phoenix, Arizona. It dates from the eighteenth century and comes from Paris. It is made of bronze with tortoiseshell inlay, which is a characteristic of Boule. Boule had two sons who carried on his tradition. They were not as intricate and did not embellish as much as their father. But this piano is by Boulle Senior.

I also have a piano-roll piano. A few years ago in Buffalo, New York, I had come across a machine for making piano-rolls which had not been used in thirty-five years. Nobody could fix it. It had fallen apart. One day, some craftsmen from Europe happened by, and, upon inspecting this machine, reckoned they could fix it. Soon it was working again.

The machine was really very primitive. You sat at a real piano, which was connected up to this machine. As you hit a key, it made a mark on a piece of paper. Subsequently, the paper was taken off and punched with a hole wherever there was a pencil mark. That became the master copy, and from it the factory could make as many other copies as were required; they could make a hundred at a time on their assembly line.

It was surprising for me to discover that there were still so many people who had player-pianos. In fact, whenever the firm puts out one of my rolls they automatically have a mail order for about 100,000. So aside from it being a nostalgic and fun thing to do, I discovered I could make money out of it. I have made about twenty rolls for them so far; and since they said I had become an expert maker of piano rolls, I thought it was about time I had a player-piano on which to play them!

So many people have asked me about my concert piano, and I am rather proud of it. There are only three in the whole world like it. And I've got all three of them!

The pianos that I now use in my work are supplied to me by Messrs Baldwin. Baldwin and I have an agreement that has lasted for over twenty years by which they design and furnish me with pianos for my stage and personal appearances as well as for television. The latest one they designed for me was made at their factory in Cincinnati. I believe it is the piano design of tomorrow. It is made of chromium and glass. The body is narrower than the standard piano, and has been manufactured for travel. It is impervious to hard shocks and knocks—and the weather!

In fact, I try to avoid any mishaps to my pianos by having all three in transit at the same time. While I'm using one piano, therefore, another is on its way to my next date. Because of their size, my pianos cannot be flown, so they are sent by truck. Thus we usually have one pianist and three pianos on tour! And all of us are tuned daily. I am always amused when people invite me over to their home and, when showing me their piano, say, "We just had it tuned, about six months ago." That is about six months too late for me.

As for my piano playing, I like to do most of my practicing at home when I am off the road. Then I practice sometimes for five or six or seven hours. Even so, there are long periods when I stay away from the piano altogether. Unless I am working on a new piece, there seems no point in just practicing exercises, lest I become stale. Often I find that two weeks of rehearsal before I go out on the road is quite sufficient. It limbers me up, so to speak.

Also I become very impatient when I'm practicing, because I want to learn the new piece right away. Sometimes, of course, it does not come that easily. Usually I listen to everybody else's version first, to make sure that I don't copy. Then I try to make my own version as authentic as anything that has been done before but, at the

84

Right, my double-keyboard piano. It's unique. And below, my piano-shaped record player.

same time, *different*. So the minute people hear my interpretation they will say, "That's Liberace." I used to practice on the road two or three hours a day in a deserted auditorium, but I found I was giving my best performances to an empty house. So now I save all my energy for the performance.

Above all, I adore the creativeness of playing the piano. I think the greatest pleasure I get is being able to create somthing that brings pleasure to others. Playing the piano is not merely for my own amusement—I never *enjoy* a number unless and until I have played it before an audience. Sometimes I feel like a painter, a painter who has created a portrait or a landscape. He himself doesn't really appreciate it until he has shown it and had it appreciated by others. There have been times, for example, when I was very high on a number and very pleased with what I created. But for some strange reason, it didn't go over with my audience. So I never played it again. I hated it. Equally, I will never do a number that I don't believe in, even if it is requested repeatedly. If that vital connection between the artist and his audience is missing, then I have failed in my job, which is essentially one of communication.

Once, I went to see Jack Benny at Lake Tahoe and loved his performance so much that I decided to pay my respects backstage. I found him lying down on a couch in his dressing room, complaining of exhaustion from all his tours and a recent European trip he had just completed. So I asked him what I had been asked many times. "Jack," I said, "since you obviously have a lot of money, why do you work so hard?" And he said that as long as people came to see him he would perform. Because when they *stopped* coming to see him and no longer enjoyed what he had to offer, then he'd shrivel up and die.

And I'm sure that is the motivating force behind my working as hard as I do. I love my work, and I love to make people happy through my work. Working in order to make a living has long passed. Let's face it, I can be just as happy with one million dollars as I can with two million dollars. As my mother often tells me, "You can only wear one suit at a time, you can only live in one house at a time, and you can only drive one car at a time!" And she's absolutely right.

But, I love doing my thing. It's not totally unselfish; it brings me great pleasure too. It brings me great satisfaction. There are times when I've felt less than a hundred percent before going out on stage. I would have given anything not to have done the show. My stomach

was upset, or I've felt I might be cheating the people because I didn't feel too good. And sometimes I have actually gone out on stage feeling terrible, with a bad cold or a virus infection, or else been terribly exhausted. But when I get out there, some kind of adrenalin is pumped into me by this desire to please and make people happy. It's a therapy for me. I've taken my mind off myself because I'm so intent on doing a good job. I'm certain now that whenever you take your mind off yourself, when you're concerned with other people, you lose yourself and become therefore a better person. Once I did an entire engagement with walking pneumonia. It was just unbelievable how I got through it. The doctor had wanted to put me in the hospital, but eventually decided that to be on stage did me more good than any medicine he could give me. Because being on stage *is* like medicine for me. And quite honestly, if that were ever taken away from me, I think I would lose the desire to live.

Incidentally, it's amazing that so many people think my name, Liberace, is a stage name. Curiously enough, earlier in my career, when I had told various promoters what my name was, they all said, "Well, we'll have to change your name because *nobody* can pronounce that." And, of course, I really did have a mouthful for a name. My first name was Walter, my middle name Valentino, and my last name really was Liberace. It was actually Paderewski's tour manager, who was also public relations director of the Statler Hilton in Washington DC, who suggested that I use only my last name. After all, Paderewski had only used his last name, and other people of his stature had done the same quite successfully. So why shouldn't I? I took his advice and soon became a one name artist.

Yet, during my early career I was often forced to use another name. I was once in a radio program called the Fitch Bandwagon, for example, when the manager of the Chicago Symphony heard me and said that, if I continued to play with this *dance* orchestra, I would forfeit my chance to play with the Symphony Orchestra. So for about six months, until the Symphony concert took place, I was known as Walter Buster Keyes, which is a terrible name. Actually, it stuck, because I soon became known as Buster to a lot of people and, to this day, I run into people who come up to me and say, "Are you that same fellow that used to play in Wisconsin called Buster Keyes?" And I have to say, "I'm afraid I am."

Maybe I went a bit too far with this room. I tell you, after a while keyboards can drive you crazy.

"Mr. Showmanship"

Not so long ago, I used to work fifty-two weeks a year, except Sundays. Now, I only work about twenty-six weeks, although, every year, it seems, I still break several box office records—including my own. The opening of the Riviera Hotel in 1955, for example, was the first time they ever paid anyone $50,000 a week in Las Vegas. Twenty years ago that was an astronomical salary. It still is. And, although, I no longer play at the Riviera, my Las Vegas salary today is still six figures.

When I'm not working, it seems, all my creative powers cease—at least, most of my ideas for stage presentation come to me while I'm actually performing. There's something about being on stage, surrounded by lights and scenery and props, that stimulates my thinking processes. Recently, while I was playing "Clair de Lune," I closed my eyes and I could see a ballerina floating around wistfully, doing some very graceful moves, interpreting the music. So when I returned to Las Vegas, I brought with me a beautiful ballerina from the Royal Ballet of London.

We usually plan my show two or three weeks ahead before the start of each tour. The music has to be selected and arranged and orchestrated—in fact, I do all my own piano arrangements before my musical director orchestrates them. And then there is the new choreography and costumes to try out. I like to begin each tour in a place where I might feel a little more relaxed, not Las Vegas or some other major city.

One of our biggest problems is trying to make the show adaptable to whatever kind of theater we finish up in, so that it will be suitable for any auditorium. This is actually more difficult than it sounds because what I perform on the Vegas stage cannot be transplanted easily into a theater-in-the-round. Sometimes I play in an area that has no curtains or back drops, for example. So I cannot plan a show that depends entirely on props or scenery or lights. In Vegas, of course, I can go all out—I can use my cars, carriages, chandeliers, statues, the spectacular dancing waters, anything. But in most of the places I play, such elaborate staging would be impossible. And that's when my costumes come into their own. My costumes are frequently the only things that set the mood—and that's now a main reason why

they have to be so spectacular. As long as *they* are eye-catching, the audience does not notice the lack of other window dressing.

I like to think that I am very well prepared, therefore, for each theater we go into. But, of course, disaster strikes occasionally—although it's usually not our fault. One time, for example, I really became angry when the place I was due to be working in had put up a temporary stage—made out of quarter-inch plywood. It was so wobbly that, when I stamped on it, my foot went straight through. I refused to go on until they had built a solid stage with curtains and drapes and flowers. I was very nearly as upset as when other people play my piano. To me, a piano is like a fountain pen. It becomes an expression of me, so I really don't like it when other people start playing me!

Left, my famous hot-pants outfit. Like many of my costumes, it began as a joke; but I soon discovered the joke gave other people pleasure besides myself, and that after all is what's important.

Rehearse, rehearse, rehearse. You can never rehearse too much or too often. To be thoroughly well prepared for a show is the mark of a true professional, and I pride myself on being just that.

Believe it or not, once upon a time both my stage presentation and my costumes were the very model of elegance and simplicity. When I started out on my television series in the early fifties, for instance, I wore a full dress suit. No sparkles at all, except, of course, for the candelabra. But in 1952, when I gave my first concert at the Hollywood Bowl before a capacity crowd of twenty thousand, I was suddenly confronted with the entire Philharmonic Orchestra—a total of a hundred and ten musicians—all dressed in black. Against this sea of black, I reckoned, my own dress suit would be completely lost. Why not wear white, I thought? And since I had already become known for my full dress suit and my tails, I had a white dress suit made with white tails!

And that is how my reputation for fancy costumes started. The columnists and critics picked it up because, believe it or not, to come on stage in 1952 in a white dress suit was quite daring. Some of them compared me to Cab Calloway, who had apparently done it before. I figured that from here on in I had better be original. There was no point in looking like Cab Calloway, or anyone else for that matter. So before long, I wore my first gold lamé and that *really* started the ball rolling.

Then Elvis Presley saw the gold suit and asked me whether he could have a gold suit made for his new movie. I was flattered and agreed. But because Elvis Presley had worn it, I had to come up with *another* idea. I tried sparkles. But they too kept on snow-balling, if you see what I mean. At first I used beads and rhinestones. Later it was sequins. I had to keep topping myself, although it was becoming more and more expensive. Finally, I had what I hoped was the ultimate idea: a jeweled suit of tails, all beaded and with diamond buttons. And the buttons spelled out my name!

On television, however, I continued to wear my black evening dress. But soon I started getting letters from people about all those suits I wore for my personal appearances. Why don't you wear them on your television show, they asked? I remember I had long drawn out meetings with my sponsors to decide whether I ought to change my image on television. I was very nervous about tampering with a

Changing costume during the show can sometimes be very frantic. Often, I have a dozen changes to make, but there's no excuse to be anything less than immaculate (as in my white tails, above right). Immediately at right is my personal costumier, Frank Acuna, who has been with me for over thirty years.

"Good evening, ladies and gentlemen and welcome to the Liberace show at the Las Vegas Hilton!"

successful format. But the sponsors insisted. So, fortified by all my fan letters, I began trying out more and more flamboyant clothes for my television series. This, of course, had one enormous disadvantage which I simply had not thought of. Once forty million people had seen a particular costume on television, it was very difficult ever to wear it again. I had to keep adding to my stockpile, therefore, and pretty soon it all became an expensive joke.

In fact, a great number of the costumes actually began life as a joke. The hotpants outfit, for instance, certainly started out like that. One time I was in San Francisco, when I was contacted by a fellow from Poland. Because of my half-Polish background, he said he'd like to make me a leather outfit. So I went to his shop and discovered he was designing and studding leather jackets in patriotic colors—red, white and blue. Now, as this was during the craze for hotpants, I got the idea of having him make me a hotpants outfit in red, white and blue, all in leather and with a little leather fringe. It seemed to me just the right outfit to wear at fancy dress parties—for fun. I would never have dreamed of wearing it in the street, unless it was covered up underneath a coat. I think I would have been too embarrassed.

One night I wore it to work—as a gag. But when all the musicians saw it, they said, "You *got* to wear that on stage; it's a *real* scream."

JOHN WAYNE

5451 Marathon Street
Hollywood, Calif. 90038
November 24, 1971

Mrs. M. Robinson
4807 Post Way
El Paso, Texas 79903

Dear Mrs. Robinson:

I have known Mr. Liberace for about
thirty years, and on many occasions
listened to him play before he became
a well-known personality.

Mr. Liberace has used his dress and
mannerisms to get the kind of publicity
that prompts "roasting" which is expected
and accepted among professional people,
as I am sure he would quickly tell you.

Please forgive me if I seem in any way
to have anything but goodwill for Mr.
Liberace.

Sincerely,

John Wayne

JW:ms

I said, "Oh, I couldn't wear that on the stage. It's just too much." But the more I thought about it, the more I realized that if my colleagues had reacted to it so favorably, then my audience would probably *love* it. After much trepidation, therefore, I decided to try it out. I had all the leather studded with rhinestones to make it sparkle, and wore it for the first time at Caesar's Palace in Las Vegas. It created a sensation.

I think the picture of me and my hotpants went all over the world. Later, when I took the hotpants on my Australian tour, we—or should I say "it"—made all the front pages. And when I returned, a charity approached me to send some of my costumes (without me in them!) on a tour raising money for muscular dystrophy. The choice of costumes was mine, they said, except that the one costume I *had* to send was my hotpants outfit. So I sent it. I understand the exhibition took in a record amount of money for the charity, which pleased me a lot.

Another outfit that had an amusing beginning was my Russian czarist costume; I used to perform an entire Russian sequence. One day someone suggested I ought to have some Russian wolfhounds as part of the act. At first I thought the idea was another joke, at my expense. But eventually I thought, "Why not?" So I started asking around and discovered I had some friends in Las Vegas who actually owned some Russian wolfhounds. "Can I rent your Russian wolfhounds?" I asked. They didn't seem at all alarmed and said yes. And then someone said, "OK, so what are you going to do *next* year? No doubt you and your dogs will drive on stage in a Rolls Royce." I said, "Why not? That's a great idea." We checked to find out whether the stage at the Hilton was strong enough to take a heavy car. It was. So on I came in my czar's costume, plus Russian wolfhounds, plus Rolls Royce. It was quite an entrance.

Right, just two of my quick changes!
As I always say, "Excuse me a
moment while I slip into something
a little more spectacular!"

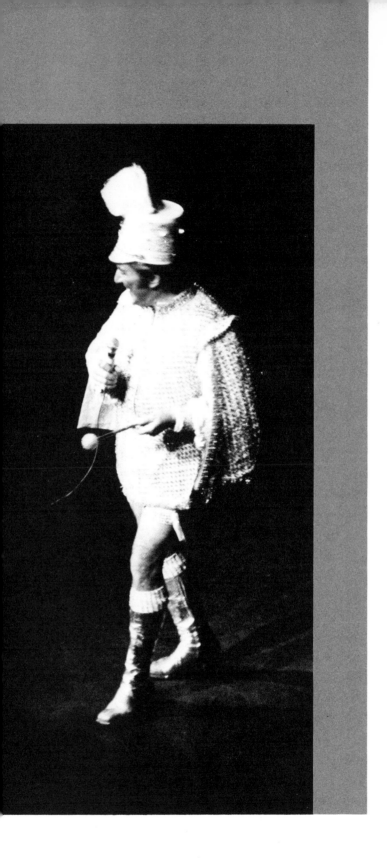

Below, me and my friend, Bertha. Unfortunately, we never really got on speaking terms. Anyway, she was bigger than me.

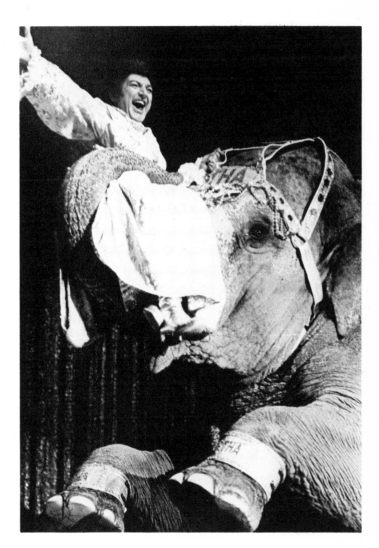

In fact, many of my stage entrances and exits also started as gags. Like flying off the stage at Las Vegas. I used to have a large cape which I wore for my final bow. One night, as I ran off stage, the cape billowed out behind me and, apparently, I looked as if I was about to become airborne. And as I came into the wings, my stage manager, Ray Arnett, said to me, "So who do you think you are? Superman or Mary Poppins?" I laughed, and then I said, "Ray, that's not such a bad idea." So I had a special flying harness made and, for my final exit, I was literally strung up. I really did become airborne!

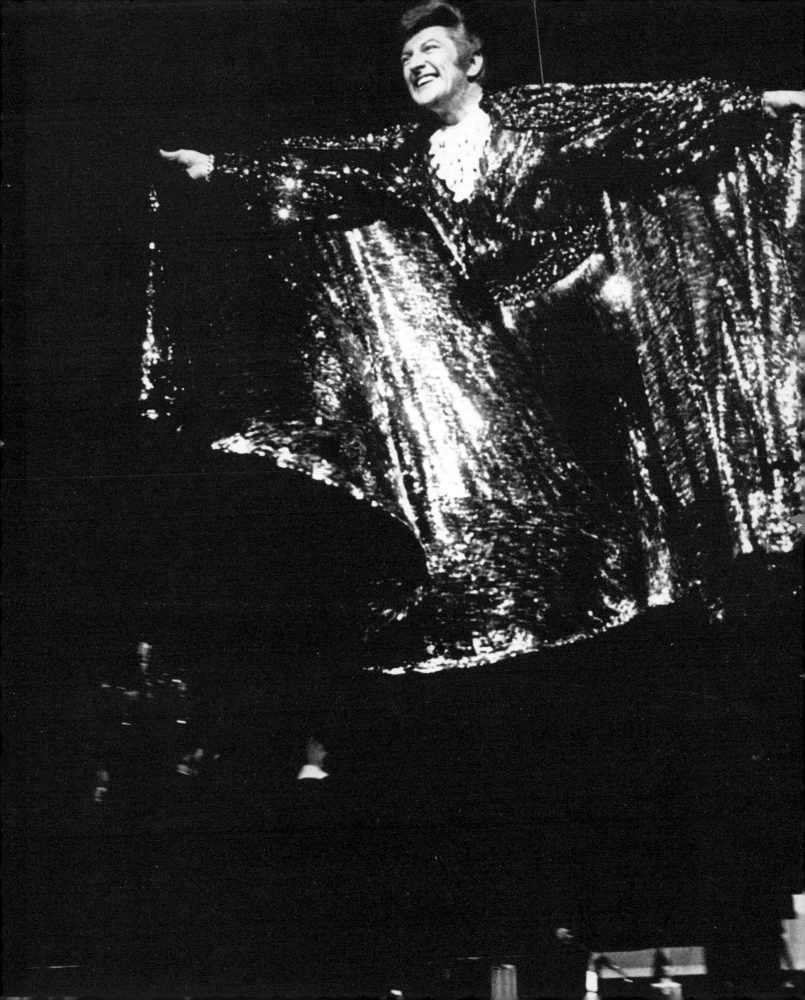

I spend an increasing amount of time at the Las Vegas Hilton, partly because Seymour, my manager, likes to sit by the pool! Seriously, I find the audiences very warm and sympathetic and the stage so well equipped. It really gives me scope to try out new ideas in my act. I used to work fifty-two weeks in the year, but now my manager insists I keep it down to around thirty. Phoenix and Warwick, Rhode Island are regulars; and then there are my friends in Canada, Australia and South Africa to think of. Not to mention Great Britain! Oh my, the list is endless. In truth, I would need one hundred weeks a year to fulfill all my obligations.

1975 Artist's Name: LIBERACE

JANUARY		MARCH		MAY		JULY		SEPT.		NOV.	
WED 1	NEW YEAR	SAT 1		THU 1		TUE 1		MON 1	Labor Day	SAT 1	
THU 2		SUN 2		FRI 2	HAMILTON	WED 2	SA HARA	TUE 2		SUN 2	
FRI 3		MON 3		SAT 3		THU 3		WED 3		MON 3	
SAT 4		TUE 4		SUN 4		FRI 4	INDEPENDENCE DAY	THU 4	WARWICK	TUE 4	
SUN 5		WED 5		MON 5		SAT 5		FRI 5		WED 5	
MON 6	OFF	THU 6		TUE 6	SASKATOON	SUN 6		SAT 6	Jewish NEW YEAR	THU 6	THU MORE
TUE 7		FRI 7		WED 7		MON 7		SUN 7	HATTING ISLAND	FRI 7	TO 6'
WED 8		SAT 8		THU 8		TUE 8		MON 8		SAT 8	
THU 9		SUN 9		FRI 9	REGINA	WED 9		TUE 9		SUN 9	WESTBURY
FRI 10		MON 10		SAT 10		THU 10		WED 10		MON 10	N.Y.
SAT 11		TUE 11		SUN 11		FRI 11		THU 11		TUE 11	
SUN 12		WED 12		MON 12		SAT 12		FRI 12		WED 12	
MON 13		THU 13		TUE 13		SUN 13		SAT 13		THU 13	
TUE 14	ARDON SHOW	FRI 14		WED 14		MON 14		SUN 14		FRI 14	
WED 15		SAT 15		THU 15		TUE 15		MON 15	YOM KIPPUR	SAT 15	
THU 16	PHOENIX	SUN 16		FRI 16	WINNIPEG	WED 16	OFF	TUE 16		SUN 16	
FRI 17	STATE TONARM	MON 17	ST PATRICK	SAT 17		THU 17		WED 17		MON 17	DALLAS?
SAT 18		TUE 18	OFF	SUN 18		FRI 18		THU 18		TUE 18	
SUN 19		WED 19		MON 19		SAT 19		FRI 19		WED 19	
MON 20		THU 20		TUE 20		SUN 20		SAT 20		THU 20	
TUE 21	OFF	FRI 21		WED 21		MON 21		SUN 21		FRI 21	
WED 22	NASHVILLE	SAT 22		THU 22		TUE 22		MON 22		SAT 22	
THU 23	ORLANDO FLA	SUN 23	PALM SUNDAY	FRI 23	OFF	WED 23		TUE 23		SUN 23	
FRI 24		MON 24		SAT 24		THU 24		WED 24		MON 24	CLEVELAND
SAT 25	ATLANTA GA.	TUE 25		SUN 25		FRI 25		THU 25		TUE 25	OHIO
SUN 26		WED 26		MON 26	MEMORIAL DAY	SAT 26		FRI 26		WED 26	
MON 27	OFF	THU 27		TUE 27		SUN 27		SAT 27		THU 27	THANKSGIVING
TUE 28	CHATTANOOGA TENN	FRI 28	GOOD FRIDAY	WED 28		MON 28		SUN 28		FRI 28	
WED 29	KNOXVILLE	SAT 29		THU 29		TUE 29		MON 29	U.V.	SAT 29	
THU 30	BIRMINGHAM	SUN 30	EASTER	FRI 30		WED 30		TUE 30		SUN 30	
FRI 31	LAKELAND FLA.	MON 31		SAT 31		THU 31					

FEB.		APRIL		JUNE		AUGUST		OCT.		DEC.	
SAT 1	ST. PETERSBURG	TUE 1		SUN 1		FRI 1		WED 1		MON 1	
SUN 2	W. PALM BEACH	WED 2	INDIANA	MON 2		SAT 2	SARATOGA N.Y.	THU 2		TUE 2	
MON 3		THU 3	COLUMBUS	TUE 3		SUN 3		FRI 3	17 WEEK	WED 3	
TUE 4		FRI 4	DAYTON	WED 4		MON 4		SAT 4		THU 4	
WED 5		SAT 5		THU 5		TUE 5		SUN 5		FRI 5	
THU 6		SUN 6		FRI 6		WED 6		MON 6		SAT 6	
FRI 7		MON 7		SAT 7		THU 7	W. SPRINGFIELD	TUE 7		SUN 7	
SAT 8		TUE 8		SUN 8		FRI 8	MASS.	WED 8		MON 8	
SUN 9		WED 9	O'KEEFE	MON 9		SAT 9		THU 9		TUE 9	
MON 10		THU 10	CENTER	TUE 10		SUN 10		FRI 10		WED 10	
TUE 11		FRI 11	TORONTO	WED 11		MON 11		SAT 11		THU 11	
WED 12	Lincoln	SAT 12		THU 12	U.V.	TUE 12	VANCOUVER	SUN 12		FRI 12	
THU 13		SUN 13		FRI 13		WED 13	NEW YORK	MON 13	COLUMBUS DAY	SAT 13	
FRI 14	LAS VEGAS	MON 14		SAT 14		THU 14		TUE 14		SUN 14	
SAT 15	HILTON	TUE 15		SUN 15		FRI 15		WED 15		MON 15	
SUN 16		WED 16		MON 16	HILTON	SAT 16		THU 16		TUE 16	
MON 17	WASHINGTON	THU 17		TUE 17		SUN 17		FRI 17		WED 17	
TUE 18	LAS VEGAS	FRI 18		WED 18		MON 18		SAT 18	DUBUQUE	THU 18	
WED 19	HILTON	SAT 19		THU 19		TUE 19		SUN 19	CASINO	FRI 19	
THU 20		SUN 20		FRI 20		WED 20		MON 20		SAT 20	
FRI 21		MON 21		SAT 21		THU 21		TUE 21		SUN 21	
SAT 22		TUE 22		SUN 22		FRI 22	?	WED 22		MON 22	
SUN 23		WED 23		MON 23		SAT 23		THU 23		TUE 23	
MON 24		THU 24	OTTAWA	TUE 24		SUN 24		FRI 24		WED 24	
TUE 25		FRI 25		WED 25		MON 25		SAT 25		THU 25	CHRISTMAS
WED 26		SAT 26		THU 26		TUE 26		SUN 26		FRI 26	
THU 27		SUN 27		FRI 27		WED 27	N. TONAWANDA	MON 27	VETERANS DAY	SAT 27	
FRI 28		MON 28		SAT 28	PALISADES PARK	THU 28	NEW YORK	TUE 28		SUN 28	
		TUE 29		SUN 29		FRI 29		WED 29		MON 29	
		WED 30	ARLINGTON	MON 30		SAT 30		THU 30		TUE 30	
						SUN 31		FRI 31		WED 31	

Seymour Heller & Associates,
Personal Management ⊕ MILWAUKEE, WISCONSIN

NORTH TONAWANDA (NEAR BUFFALO)

A DIVISION OF AMERICAN VARIETY INTERNATIONAL, INC.
9220 Sunset Boulevard, Suite 224 • Los Angeles, California 90069 • (213) 273-3060

Presentation is everything in a stage performance. There would be no point in arriving dressed in jeans and a shirt, would there?

I love the people to see my rings and jewels at the end of a performance. After all, they bought them! As I always say, "See what you can get if you practice!"

I have no idea how many costumes I have altogether. I suppose I must have over five hundred. The heaviest one, curiously enough, is that self-same hotpants outfit. Or rather, its twin brother. I had another version made, complete with a jacket and top hat patterned after a band major's costume of the John Philip Sousa era, which was completely electrified. With the flick of a switch, I could light up nearly four thousand miniature lights sown into the fabric. It was a spectacular effect—I looked like a walking Christmas tree—but it weighed forty-three pounds, and I needed two men to help me into it. Once you had it on, you felt like a human hanger! The top part of the jacket had wings on it, and even the hat lit up. But it was the weight that I found exhausting. The costumes that *look* the heaviest, oddly enough, are sometimes the lightest ones, but *anything* that has jewels or beads on it becomes heavy. And we all know how much I love jewels and beads!

Over the years, of course, my costumes have become steadily more and more bizarre. Admittedly, what I wore twenty years ago was thought to be the ultimate in flamboyance. But today those clothes would go unnoticed. Thanks to all this glitter rock we're going through, with Elton John and Gary Glitter and Alice Cooper, for my costumes to remain the ultimate in flamboyance they have to be expensively done. Years ago I could get away with things that were not costly. Now, because of the extremes I have to indulge in to make my costumes really outstanding, they have become truly expensive. Sometimes I look at all this stuff and I can hardly believe what I have to spend. Oh well. My clothes may look funny, but they're making me money.

Yet I try to keep abreast of fashion. I had a costume made of denim not so long ago when denim was in vogue, although, of course, being me, I had it jeweled—to make it sparkle! I also like to embellish on what I've done before. Instead of just having the Royal coach and the Royal robes for my entrance in Las Vegas (that was *last* year!), next time I shall have white horses pulling the Royal coach. Horses on stage! That will shock 'em. Nothing is impossible, especially in Vegas.

Many of my ideas for stage presentation and costumes are taken from history books. My costumier, Frank Acuna, also has a wealth of material from the motion pictures he has costumed. In his time, he has worked with many of the great stars of motion pictures, all the way back to Rudolph Valentino, John Barrymore, and Frederic March. My costume with the diamond buttons, for example, has a cape with it that is a copy of the one Frederic March wore in "Anthony Adverse." I also have a costume that is an exact replica of an Argentinian gaucho costume Frank made for Rudolph Valentino. The only change in *my* version, however, is that Frank has embroidered it a little! The original, I fancy, was more . . . conservative.

Some years ago, when I was antiquing in London, I came across two magnificent signed lithographs of the Coronation of King George V. One showed King George V in his coronation regalia (it has the Royal Crest on the frame), and the other, Queen Mary in her queenly robes and gown. That too has the Royal Crest. Later, I discovered these pictures had hung originally in Buckingham Palace.

I also came across a scrapbook that had been kept by Queen Victoria of all the fox hunts she attended. It was a marvellous photographic diary of the reign of Queen Victoria and contained signatures of all the Royal guests. I asked the lady in the antique shop why these articles were no longer in the possession of the Royal Family. And she explained that there is so much memorabilia connected with the Royal Family that from time to time they have a clear out. Things that seem so precious to other people, are treated as junk by the Royal Household. Anyway, I bought the scrapbook and the pictures and hung the latter in my home in Palm Springs.

Then, one day I was looking at the picture of King George, when suddenly it occurred to me that it would be magnificent if I had a costume made exactly like his. But I was quite sure that all the fur and ermine would be prohibitively expensive, so I did nothing about it. Until, that is, a very dear friend of mine called Judy Bailey (her husband owned two hotels in Las Vegas—the Hacienda and the New Frontier) died of cancer, leaving me in her will a chinchilla coat which I had often admired. It was a full length chinchilla. Jokingly,

Above, me as Rudolph Valentino. You will remember that my mother had a passion for the great movie star, so named me Valentino, and my brother Rudolph.

I had often said, "Well, Judy, if you ever get tired of that coat, I'd really love to have it." She told me it had cost sixty thousand dollars!

So, now, all of a sudden, I had the perfect fur which could be used for my Royal King George V robe. I went to Frank Acuna with my Buckingham Palace picture and said, "Frank, make me one of these!" And he did. First we looked around for fabrics out of which to make the basic costume. I searched all over and finally came across some imported velvet in royal blue. I had all the lining jeweled and the robe embroidered with silver embroidery. But the final touch, and the element which gave the robe its true regal splendor, was the chinchilla.

My street clothes are, perhaps, a little more . . . restrained. I'm sure the reason I love so many clothes is because when I was a kid I had to wear my brother George's hand-me-downs! Now that I can afford to buy my own, however, I need them in various shapes and sizes be-

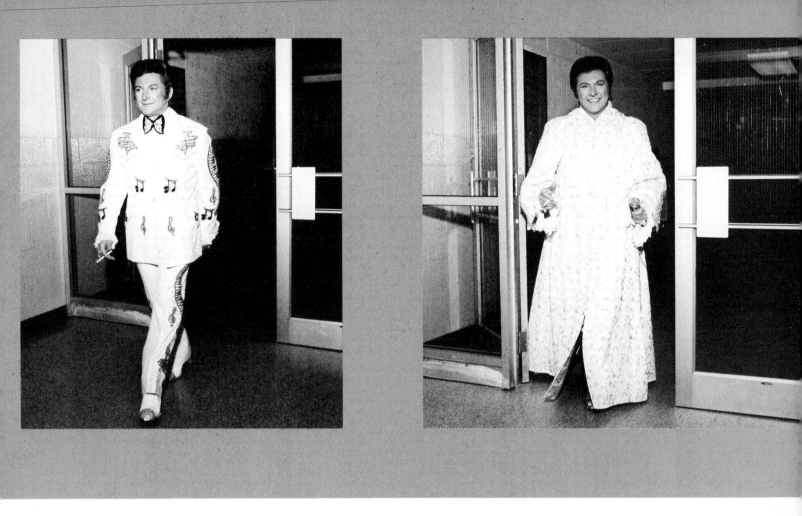

cause I love to eat and my weight fluctuates. Most of my suits, for example, come in three varieties—thin, fat, and impossible. I have them in a see-through wardrobe with sliding glass doors. In my Los Angeles house I have about two hundred suits, four hundred sports shirts and slacks, and about a hundred pairs of shoes. And, believe it or not, I have worn them all.

But even some of my street clothes have the strangest origins. Once, when I was in Rome, someone sent me to a top tailor for a suit I could wear for television interviews. The tailor obliged by showing me all his samples, but they seemed terribly conservative. I kept saying I wanted something that was outstanding! All the things he kept offering me were so bland. After all, I said, I am *noted* for my clothes. But he persisted and kept bringing out book after book of the same boring samples. Eventually, in despair, he admitted that he

didn't understand what I had in mind. I said, "Well, something with color, like your draperies." "So you like the draperies in the window?" he asked. "Yes," I said. "In that case, I will make you a suit out of the draperies." And that is exactly what he did. He got some more of the same material and made me a suit out of the draperies. It was a sensation. The only one in the world!

Another time, when I was in Philadelphia, I went to one of my favorite men's shops called the Côte d'Azur. Again, I said I wanted something . . . unusual. The manager brought out all their suits, but again they seemed to me altogether predictable. Then I noticed that the plastic couch on which I was sitting was covered with the weirdest of fabrics. "I *love* this material on the couch," I said. "Who did it for you?" The shop assistant replied that he thought he could get some more if I really liked it as much as I appeared to. "I want a suit made out of *that*," I said. And so they made me a suit out of this upholstery material which turned out to be *fantastic*. Every time I wore this particular suit, therefore, I could boast that it had left a terrific hole in their couch!

Sometimes, of course, my enthusiasms turn out to be a little expensive. When the denim craze was at its height, for example, I bought a beaded, handpainted and jeweled denim jacket in Dallas which had been made from recycled pieces of prisoners' denim. It was decorated with Texas oil wells and even had a hole (for the oil well) in it. Typically, I forgot to ask how much it was. When I was told it cost $595 I had a fit. I complained about the hole, but they said, "Why? That makes it look really authentic!" Anyway, I bought it.

It gave me the idea, however, that it might be fun if more people had studded, jeweled Levis. At first, everyone was skeptical. (This was ten years ago). "You could get away with it," they said, "but no one else will." But as soon as I started to wear the oil well in public, it caused a sensation and everybody wanted one. "Where did you get it?" they asked. "I have just got to get one like that." They all wanted it.

The street clothes and the stage clothes frequently overlap, of course. Once I went to a shop in London's Carnaby Street which stocked old uniforms that had come out of the Admiralty, uniforms for special occasions, such as when the Royal Family was present. I bought a whole bunch of them, not really for the uniforms, but for their gold braid. I brought them back and had all the gold braid cleaned. My costumier, Frank Acuna, said that gold braid was almost a lost art because the cost of it had become prohibitive. But here I had tons of it. So Frank salvaged all the gold braid he could and used it on some new costumes! The denuded uniforms then made excellent material for some street suits.

I have to admit that clothes have always fascinated me. Early in my career, for instance, I used to play for fashion shows. Often I would bring home one of the sample gowns and give it to my sister, or I'd find a beautiful cape or gown for my mother. It got to the point where they *never* bought any clothes for themselves; they'd just wait for me to bring what I had chosen. When it came to an opening night, moreover, both my mother and my sister would say, "Well, *you* pick something for us to wear." And as my career developed, people who knew I was "interested" in fashion would come to me with their latest design and say, "This is something new. Maybe your sister would like to try it?"

One time I did a fashion show for Mike Douglas in which there was one particular dress that I thought would suit my sister Angie perfectly. "The only thing is," I said, "it's a bit too shapely and my sister is not that well-endowed." "Never mind," said the fashion co-ordinator. "Neither is the model. She's wearing an inflatable bra under her dress and that's what gives her that beautiful figure." So I said, "What's an inflatable bra?" And she said, "Well, it's like a regular bra, but you can inflate it to make it any size you want. You can be voluptuous, or you can be semi-voluptuous." I said, "I gotta get Angie one of those bras!" So I got one and gave it to Angie and Angie thought it was the greatest. When she inflated it she had curves all of a sudden where before she'd never had curves.

About this time we were going on a tour to Australia; Angie used to travel with me to look after my costumes. We got on the plane— and this was several years ago before planes were pressurized as they are today—and after we were airborne, Angie put her seat back and proceeded to take a little nap. After a while I looked over at her out of the corner of my eye and noticed that her chest was getting larger and larger and larger. She was really going . . . up. Soon everyone was staring at her. Then one side of the bra deflated; it had gotten too big and burst! So there she was with one breast enormous, while the other was now flat-chested. I woke her up and said, "Angie, you'd better run to the ladies room quick. Something has happened to your bra."

Occasionally these things get out of hand.

So much for my clothes. Another essential part of my stage presentation, of course, is my jewelry. Usually I wear most of my jewelry, partly because I believe if you can't wear it you shouldn't have it. My collection, however, was originally started by people for whom I worked. Much of it was given me by sponsors or those in my organization. In fact, they say I'm a very hard person to buy things for, although I can't see why. I don't think you can *ever* have too many diamonds. I've gotten into Indian jewelry lately, which I've discovered is not only interesting but very expensive. Anyone like to give me some Indian jewelry? It's all insured, of course, although one time in Dallas I had some pieces which happened to be new and, therefore uninsured, stolen from my hotel room. Luckily, because all my jewelry is so distinctive and so personalized, the FBI was able to trace the missing items to a fence in Chicago who had made the great mistake of wearing a particular ring of mine which was instantly identifiable. They took out a warrant against him and subsequently uncovered five hundred thousand dollars worth of other stolen jewelry. I became a hero because of my jewels! So nowadays I wear all my jewelry. It makes me feel secure!

Well, not always. I was travelling once with Scottie Plummer, the banjo player, when his mother wanted to take him over to see some city just inside Canada. We drove across the border, shopped for a few hours and then drove back. On our return, I was sitting in the rear of the car. As we came to the US customs, the officer said, "Did you buy those in Canada?" Thinking the man was joking, I said, "Not hardly" or something. "OK, mister," the man said. "Would you get out of the car?" They held me three or four hours, awaiting identification!

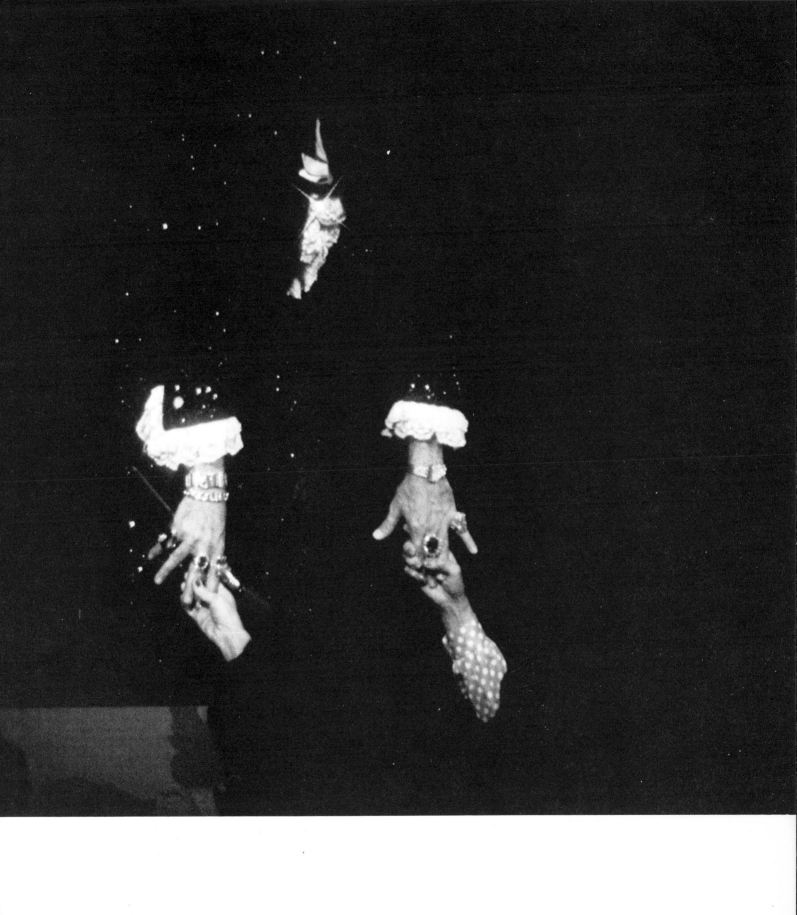

I mentioned my Rolls Royce which I used for my Russian entrance at Las Vegas. In fact, I collect cars—again primarily for my stage presentation, but also for fun.

The most elaborate vehicle in my collection is in fact my custom-built Rolls Royce limousine. It's the most elaborate, and also the most expensive. There were only a few of these built because the thing that makes it so special is the Landau top.

Car number two is a custom-built Cadillac limousine designed by Durham. There were two of these cars made; the other was a bullet-proof model designed for Ladybird Johnson when Lyndon B. Johnson was President of the United States. It has some unusual appointments on the inside. I had a bar designed, for example, by a coach crafter who usually works on Rolls Royces. Again, it's quite unique.

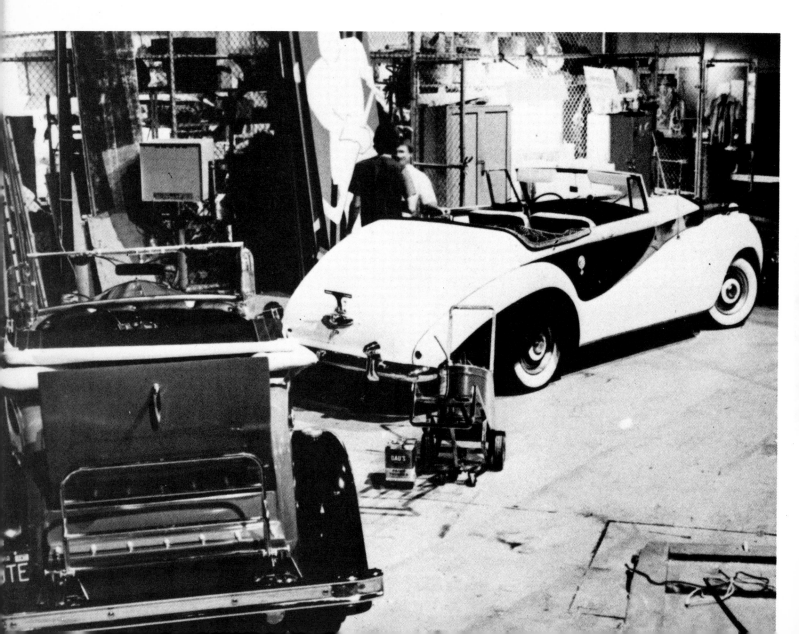

Above, my sports car, thirties-style. Actually, it's an Excalibur.

Left, the car I most like to drive myself about in, parked outside the front of my Hollywood house.

Above, my Rolls Royce limousine with the landau top. Right, something a little older!

The inside of my custom-built Cadillac, complete with a bar which was built for me by Coachcraft. Even I need to stretch my legs after a hectic day. Below—removals! Overleaf is my London taxi, which has certain modifications, as you can see.

And this is car number three. This is an English taxi cab. It's of 1957 vintage. I bought it in London and had it shipped to the States. I changed the color because the English cabs are black. I had the floor carpeted in red carpeting, and the meter still works in the old English coinage of pounds, shillings and pence.

In all I have fifteen cars and one on the way. Not long ago I came to the conclusion that I ought to put this little sign up somewhere in my home. "The difference between men and boys is the price of their toys." How do you like that?

Yesterday, Today, and Forever

A few times in my life I've told myself I needed to get away from it all—go someplace where nobody knew me and take a real good rest, where there would be no one who was going to want my autograph. In fact, I tried a couple of journeys like that, but after a few days I found it terribly disappointing. I caught myself telling people who I was, simply because I was not getting the treatment to which I had become accustomed. I'm used to walking in a restaurant and being shown to the best table and receiving the best service. But suddenly all this had stopped. I had become just another person.

138

Once, I was even refused admittance to a restaurant in Greece because the headwaiter said I was not properly dressed. I did not have a shirt and tie, he said. (Actually, I had a very attractive outfit on. It was a real nice sports coat which I thought looked very nautical.) "I'm sorry," he said. "You will have to wear a shirt and a tie." So I found myself saying, "Don't you know who I am?" I felt I was only speaking up for my rights!

So I've decided now that really I do not enjoy being unrecognized. As long as I have a choice, I would rather be recognized than not. Anyway, whenever I go outside into department stores or restaurants, people *do* recognize me . . . and I love it.

But it's not all self-satisfaction. There is another, and more important, reason. The longer I stay in this business, the more I realize that we need people—not just because they buy tickets for my concerts, but because of the love they provide. In my own career, the real turning point came when I first appeared on television. It seemed that all the struggle, all those years of having people learn how to pronounce my name, had been forgotten. Almost overnight, as soon as I had begun my syndicated television series, the name Liberace and its pronunciation became commonplace. Little children used to come up to me and say, "Hello Liberace." It was a revelation because, to be perfectly honest, I couldn't pronounce the name *myself* until I was about 13.

I confess that this need to be acknowledged and applauded has always been very strong in me. One night, while I was still appearing

at the Waldorf Astoria in the early fifties, I had gone into a Third Avenue bar and discovered it had one of those "soundy" machines, which was a primitive, visual juke box. You dialled a record, and got a short, talking movie. I had done a couple of these soundies myself when I had first arrived in New York. Each lasted for about three minutes; one was "12th Street Rag," and the other "Tiger Rag." All I had done was sit and play surrounded by a lot of pretty girls, while the movie people filmed me.

Anyway, upon investigation I discovered that my own records were on this particular machine. I gave the bartender a couple of quarters and asked him to put on "12th Street Rag," which he did. And then I had the satisfaction of noticing all these so-called derelicts and drunks discover me actually sitting at their bar! I was the same person they could now see on their movie screen. That night I felt I had truly arrived! I was being recognized in this very simple place by the people, who needless to say, treated me with a lot of attention. They bought me drinks and more drinks until I walked out floating on a cloud. I know many performers in show business who are unable to cope with being recognized—some who even prefer to remain anonymous, as far as that is possible. All I can say is that, for me, being known and being successful beats obscurity to hell.

The difference between being recognized by the man on the street, moreover, as opposed to high society is very important to me. The old saying that God must have loved the common man because he made so many of them, seems particularly true about the people who have made Liberace what he is today.

When I began my television career, I was taught a great lesson. The man who produced my first TV show invited me to dinner one night to discuss our future programs. Later, we drove out through Beverly Hills and Hollywood, past all those beautiful homes. But my producer insisted that we go on, past endless suburban houses and into the mobile home areas. Then, he stopped and asked me a single question. "What do you see here," he said, "that you didn't see in Beverly Hills?" After thinking a while, I said, "Television aerials." "Yes," he said. *"That's* your audience!" He said that if I could please *those* people, I had it made. "Don't worry about the inhabitants of Beverly Hills," he said. "They will come to you— in time."

I am sure now, looking back over my career, that café society would never have supported me this long. After all, I have been in

On the road, or at least in the air, with my stage manager, Ray Arnett.

show business for thirty years. Upper class audiences are fickle. They are always looking for that latest thrill in entertainment. I think for them the "thrill" of Liberace would have worn off a long time ago.

I suppose I *could* have been happy earning a comfortable salary and being acknowledged by a handful of café society followers. But I know that wouldn't have satisfied me for long. Anyway, I was never sure whether I was doing the right thing—musically or entertainment-wise—until television came into my life. Before long, I was being seen by twenty or thirty million people. I became known to so many people that it convinced me at last that I was fulfilling myself.

Coping with my sudden success, moreover, was no problem. Indeed, I've always felt sorry for those entertainers who found themselves unable to adjust. And there are many—not just the new crop of entertainers, but some of the real old timers—who could not cope. They had so many personal hang-ups or unhappy episodes or marriages or associations in their private lives, that they were not able to deal with the other life they had created. I speak of the Judy Garlands of this world. Often, it's the question of privacy. Yet it seems to me obvious that the moment you become public property, you forfeit a certain amount of personal privacy. This is something which all entertainers must face. I suppose the fact that I started my career so early

I've always known the importance of pleasing the fans, as here at the beginning of my career, with brother George. After all, they have made me what I am, and I want them to know I'm grateful.

in life and struggled for so many years as a nonentity—even if I was a "successful unknown"—helped me. When recognition came, it was so refreshing and so different that I revelled in it.

Twenty years ago I was called television's first matinee idol. But always in the back of my mind was that old adage, "Here today and gone tomorrow." "How long is this going to last?" I kept asking myself. Now, after all this time, I do seem to have created a career for myself that has all the assurance of longevity. So a very frequent question I am asked is, "When are you going to retire? Because now you have everything." Being a success, however, does not mean the acquisition of a whole heap of material things, such as houses or cars or clothes or jewels. It means being able to return the love that other people have given you.

Of course, the most obvious way in which your audience expresses that love is by writing to you. I *often* get letters from people who are madly in love with me! Several years ago, a lawyer actually called my office to say that a Miss So-and-So was divorcing her husband and coming out to marry me! Another woman wrote four or five letters a day. She called me her husband and signed herself Mrs. Liberace. Then she called up my mother and addressed her as mother-in-law! She even sent birthday cards and Mother's Day cards. That is the kind

Meeting the Queen Mother at my third Royal Variety Performance in the London Palladium, October 30, 1972. With me are Danny la Rue, the British female impersonator, and Carol Channing.

STARTED TO PLAY PIANO AT THE AGE OF 4, THE GREAT PADEREWSKI, A GOOD FRIEND OF THE FAMILY, WAS THE ONE WHO SUGGESTED THAT THE YOUNG PIANIST DROP HIS FIRST TWO NAMES AND BECAME KNOWN AS LIBERACE . . . . .

MADE HIS DEBUT WITH CHICAGO SYMPHONY ORCHESTRA AT 16. HIS DEAR MOTHER IS ALWAYS ON HAND AND HE INTRODUCES HER TO AUDIENCES WHENEVER THE OPPORTUNITY ARISES, RECALLING THE TIME WHEN SHE WORKED 16 HOURS A DAY TO HELP SUPPORT THEIR FAMILY AND PAY FOR MUSIC LESSONS, ALSO FOR BROTHER GEORGE AND SISTER ANGIE . . .

Liberace
KLAC-TV • Channel 13
WAS BORN UNDER THE SIGN OF TAURUS IN MILWAUKEE OF AN ITALIAN FATHER AND POLISH MOTHER.

HAS COME A LONG WAY SINCE HIS FIRST JOB PLAYING MUSICAL ACCOMPANIMENT FOR SILENT MOVIES IN MILWAUKEE SCHOOLS; HAS BEEN ACCLAIMED ON CONCERT STAGES BOTH IN THE U.S. AND EUROPE; MADE HIS BIGGEST HOLLYWOOD HIT AT A RECENT ENGAGEMENT AT CIRO'S. LIBERACE AND HIS BROTHER GEORGE, AN EXCELLENT MUSICIAN IN HIS OWN RIGHT, AND ALSO HIS MUSICAL DIRECTOR, ARE GREAT PALS. LIBERACE IS ALSO QUITE AN ARTIST WITH A BRUSH AND IN THE KITCHEN, SPECIALIZING IN FOREIGN FOODS.

of love I can do without. Another woman used to send $300, maybe two or three times a year. We didn't want to take the money, but we had no way of returning it. So we gave it all to charity.

All letters are a lifeline to your audience. But I still get hurt when I receive unflattering letters, people commenting adversely on my stage performance or on my pianos and silly clothes. And I am always getting letters from people who want things; one woman sent a letter saying she needed me to pay for her stay in a diet home. She weighed 300 pounds and wanted to lose weight. She also wanted me to pay for someone to take care of her children while she was away!

Another time I had a letter from a woman who had become pregnant (she said) because I had looked at her! If I remember correctly, she/we had twin sons. Once, a home for wayward girls in Chicago wrote asking me to furnish them a piano because some poor girl had gotten mad and had broken up their own. I get at least two requests a week for pianos.

I suppose I'm the type of person that people think will be easy to take advantage of. Everybody, it seems, who has a charity bazaar expects me to make an appearance. Obviously, I appreciate being written to. Yet I would never *expect* anyone to do anything for me without first asking them. Not to do so would be like breaking an unspoken trust.

Anyway, fan mail simply goes on increasing and increasing. Fifteen years ago I used to get several bags of mail per week. Now I get over two hundred letters a day. Christmas cards? Oh, well over a thousand, mostly from people I have never met. One old lady sends me a box—every Christmas time—full of either dead roses or a switch she has worn in her hair or her children's toys, anything that has meant a lot to her.

I also get sent cakes and pies and fudge. I don't eat any of it, of course, because you can never be too sure what has been put inside. And ties—you should see some of the ties I get! They're outrageous! But I know that the people who send them meant well, so I've learned to keep smiling, whatever arrives in the post.

Fan clubs are another means by which an artist keeps in touch with his audience, and in particular with his most loyal fans. There was a time—in the early forties, for example, when a singer like Sinatra was becoming popular—when fan clubs were essential in order for you to achieve international status. When I started out in the early fifties, moreover, fan clubs were still very important to ensure

There's no escaping autograph hunters. Well, sometimes you just have to grin and bear it.

the continued popularity of the artist. In fact, my first fan club had been started in 1947, and I used to contribute money for postage and bulletins. Pretty soon, my fan clubs began to mushroom and develop in other parts of the world, and they *all* needed contributions to sustain their memberships. It got to be a very expensive item.

But, since the advent of television, these fan clubs are no longer as important. Fan mail, however, is different. It comes direct from the general public, the people that you have actually reached, rather than the people who have selected themselves to be your followers. If I had had to depend on members of my fan clubs, moreover, I don't think

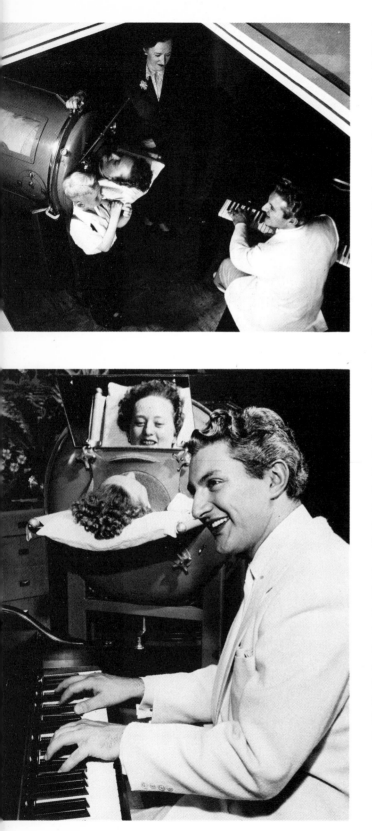

I would be in the business today. After all, I crave for a much more general acceptance of my work, which the mail which I receive now demonstrates. I have lonely hearts; I have lunatics; I have people who think I am the richest pianist in the world and want a handout; I have religious fanatics; I have everybody.

I also have a great number of letters from sensible people who write me with sincerity about quite mundane problems that exist in their daily life. They feel I can help them or contribute in some way, and not just with money. In fact, many people turn to me for advice —I don't know why—but even my closest friends have come to regard me as an unpaid psychiatrist. Perhaps the most important reason why they seek me out is that I seem to have an outward, happy countenance. I don't seem to be burdened with any problems. I am always smiling and happy and always try to be kind to people. I never allow myself to be grouchy.

This was brought home to me once very painfully in Chicago. While I was doing my television series, I used to receive letters from a lady by the name of Mary Kitzmüller. She told me she was confined to an iron lung because of polio, but she had never missed my television shows. So the next time I went to Chicago, I arranged to give a private concert for her in her home. The studio sent over a piano and I gave her a little recital. Then, because I mentioned this visit later on my television series, all her neighbors got together and raised enough money to buy her a special home with ramps so that she could be wheeled around easily from one room to another. A few months later, she had made such wonderful progress that she was allowed out of her iron lung for the first time in years and came to see me in Chicago at one of my concerts. She stayed for the whole of the concert. It was a truly wonderful display of courage which has left its mark on me ever since. The pictures show me playing for her.

Her strength, moreover, reminded me of the almost unbelievable burdens that some people in this world have to carry. On the other hand, if you were to analyze the letters I am sent, you would find that much of the sorrow which exists is brought about by the individuals themselves. I think it is essential, therefore, to have a positive approach to life, whether you are a pianist or a bricklayer or a senator. As long as you do your work with sincerity and dedication, as well as a happy outlook on life, you can avoid many unhappy burdens. I have no doubt that if I concentrated on adversity, I would find a lot of things to bug me and weigh heavily on my mind. But it would be such a drain on my energies, that I purposely avoid it. No one can

Above, with Pope Pius XII, Rome, 1952. Left, playing for Mary Kitzmüller, who could only see me from her iron lung by looking in a mirror.

claim to have conquered the whole world! Yet many of the problems in the world today stem from hate. And perhaps I am more conscious of it than most because I am surrounded by so much love.

I know, of course, that you can't ignore reality. In fact, I counteract it in various ways. During the resignation speech of President Nixon, for instance, I was performing in Baltimore. The theater manager came to me and asked if I would announce the President's decision on stage. I said, "Absolutely not. It would be a downer, and I am here to entertain people not depress them. If the audience is interested enough to know what President Nixon has to say tonight, they can go home and watch the telecast. But I don't want that kind of cloud hanging over *my* shoulder." So I refused to make any announcement.

Yet I frequently get depressed myself about events that happen in the world, whether they be natural disasters or personal tragedies. I am deeply affected by them, partly because I am acutely sensitive to disasters. My work is a great therapy. I lose myself for those couple of hours and try to forget. I am very grateful, therefore, for the opportunity to work so hard and so consistently.

The longer I stay in this business, however, the more I realize how little I have accomplished. Certainly, the world is becoming a smaller place through advances in the technological age such as the miracle of aviation. Yet I find there is still so much that I *haven't* accomplished, so many countries I haven't been to.

On the other hand, I never go on stage to preach. I do my thing, and I do it sincerely. I *want* the audience to love me; and the only way to do that is to let them know that I care about them and love *them*. I sometimes wonder what would happen if I planted a different seed (which I have seen other performers do), a seed wherein you incite riot and disorder. If only you could get an audience all thinking one way, and thus create a feeling of congeniality, you could dispel many of the world's problems. I rarely let things bother me too much. When I left that hospital in Pittsburgh where I almost died, I thought to myself that if I ever got out of that place alive I'd never complain again. It was as simple as that.

People don't realize how truly lucky they are just to have their health and to be blessed with good and loyal friends. And if you have the added pleasure of being surrounded by material beauty, as I have been over the past few years, then one is really fortunate. I can honestly say that I count my blessings—every day.

The Cloisters

Those of my friends who have been to all my homes feel most comfortable at the house in Palm Springs. In the Hollywood house, some of them tell me, they experience a certain coldness; they are often afraid to sit down for fear of damaging anything! But here, in Palm Springs, because of my dogs and everything, visitors feel more relaxed. Anyway, much of the furniture—especially in the family room—is really indestructible. Even the dogs can't hurt it. The furniture is covered in hide, for example, and the flooring is grass carpeting.

It's strange, you know, acquiring another house; sometimes it's like going out shopping. In my travels I often see something I don't have, especially nowadays when so many young people are becoming experts in unusual crafts. Once, I was in the Mall at Palm Springs when I noticed that someone had gotten the idea of taking bits of mirror and turning them into fantastic pictures for wall decorations. I bought one that looked just like a sunburst. Another represented the Taj Mahal, but all done with mirrors. What really attracted me, however, was that, whereas most people who have art displays put up a sign saying "Please do not touch," in the mirror booth there was a sign which read "Please touch." And that is precisely the feeling—"please touch"—that has influenced me in decorating my house in Palm Springs.

Most of the time I am attracted by anything that makes me smile. I feel that if it makes me smile, it might make other people smile. Maybe it's a cute little ceramic or a pair of love birds or a set of porcelain dogs. Just little things that when you look at them amuse you. After all, many of the objects you see in my houses are not that valuable, but they do have a certain cheerfulness about them which I hope rubs off. Some of my possessions, of course, are priceless, and I admit they give me great pleasure also. But having things about you that you are afraid to touch is no fun at all. If something gets knocked over and broken, it's not the end of the world, is it?

My house in Palm Springs, which is called The Cloisters, is considered historical by American standards. It dates back to 1925, which is old for American houses; more or less any house over fifty years old is usually condemned and torn down.

The house, when I first saw it, was a hotel, a small hotel; it had thirty-two guest rooms, and was crying out to be saved. It had decayed noticeably and was actually going to be demolished—not because it was ready to fall down or because it was dangerous to walk through, however, but because of its terrible reputation. It had been designed originally as a beautiful hall. Later, its first owners had added wings, and it had become a guest ranch. Then, as time went on, like all homes, it began to need attention. But instead of putting more money into it, the owners had sold it.

The next owners decided that, to keep people going there during their winter holidays, they would have to lower its rates to make it a little more . . . inviting. But in lowering the rates, they attracted a lower clientele and, pretty soon, it was just a cheap motel. You could rent a room, no questions asked, anytime, no luggage or anything. The fact that the motel was between the Catholic church and the Jewish synagogue didn't help. People from both organizations became concerned, and eventually got together a petition to turn the site into a parking lot.

I heard about it through one of its former owners who had lived there back in its heyday. She called me and said, "Don't let them destroy this house. It has such memories. You of all people could make it beautiful again, could make it one of the highlights of Palm Springs. Like it used to be." So I came to see it, fell in love with it, and since it seemed such a good investment, bought it.

Everyone expected I was going to tear it down and build a new home on the site. They were very, very surprised, therefore, when I

began to restore it. In fact, I was able to save about sixty percent of the original. The ceilings and the floors, those are all original. So is the gallery. I saved the tower. That's the original tower. So are most of the tiles on the roof, although many were broken. The main roof leaked like a sieve. I had all the tiles removed, the original tiles that is, had each of them individually repaired and then replaced them one at a time. It cost close to $400,000 to restore the whole house, but it was worth it.

And most of the new things which I have added I tried to make look as if they had always been there.

For a long time I wondered why the house was called The Cloisters. Many people thought that, being across from the Catholic church, this must have been the place where certain members of the church lived. But I discovered this wasn't true. In fact, to this day I do not know the origin of the name.

Nonetheless, I figured that if the house was called The Cloisters, it ought to look like one. So I created a cloister garden and, at one end, built a chapel from what was the motel snack bar. Apparently there used to be a little house at the end of the garden in which there were all kinds of soft drink dispensers, as well as cigarette and Seven-Up and peanut machines. I took everything out and turned it into a semi-enclosed chapel, complete with stained glass windows. All the appointments I collected from old churches I had visited in my travels, from Spain to Philadelphia. The large stained glass window, for example, is from Rhode Island. Most remarkable of all, however, is the statue of St. Anthony, which comes from Italy. When I found it, it had been coated with many layers of paint. But, characteristically, I decided to clean it up a little only to discover that it was actually a wood carving dating back to the sixteenth century.

I'm not always so lucky, of course, especially when it comes to wooden statues. Several years ago, before I came to Palm Springs, while in Cincinnati I stumbled across another carving of an apostle. Some of the fingers were broken off, however, and that kind of bothered me, so I offered the dealer $50 for it. He was very adamant and insisted on having $60. The following year, I noticed the statue was still there so I teased him about it. "You still have that old beat up statue?" And he said, "Sixty dollars." And I said, "Fifty." It got to be a joke.

But the third year I went back the statue was gone. I said, "So you finally sold that beat up statue?" He took me to his office, and, pinned up on his walls, was the story of the statue. He had sold it to a lady in Tennessee who had taken it to a museum, which had had it authenticated. It was one of the missing apostles from a collection in Spain that dated back to the fifteenth century. She had then sold it for $18,500 to the Metropolitan Museum of Art in New York, which had valued it at something like $275,000 and put it in a special room all by itself. And I could have bought it for a mere $60!

I asked this fellow who had only wanted $60 for it how he felt about having let a treasure slip through his fingers. He said, "It only goes to prove we have bargains." Even so, his business had increased enormously because of the publicity. There were now hordes of people rummaging through his place for bargains or treasures. He had had to buy the building next door and now owns a five story antique shop in Cincinnati!

The experience, however, taught me something important. Now, whenever I suspect that an antique I have come across might be valuable—like the statue of St. Anthony—I seek advice. I called in an appraiser from the Los Angeles museum about the St. Anthony, for example, and asked him what he thought I had. He made extensive tests and told me, first of all, that the statue was not plaster but wood. Subsequently, he proved that it was not only very old but probably worth many thousands. I had learned my lesson.

So when I discovered the desk which now sits in my bedroom at Palm Springs, I knew I had a treasure. In fact, the desk was so beautiful that when I bought it I didn't care whether it was authentic or not. If anyone had gone to so much trouble to make such an extraordinary reproduction, I thought, it had to be valuable even as a reproduction.

Nonetheless, I had it authenticated just to be certain what it was. It turned out to be a desk that had been given to Czar Nicholas II of Russia and, on it, the Franco-Russian alliance had been signed. It dated back to Louis XV and had taken four and a half years to make. All its bronzes were signed Claudet—Claudet was one of the great bronze workers of the eighteenth century. It is now insured for $275,000.

Another interesting feature of the desk was that it seemed full of tiny holes. I thought that worms might have gotten into it, so I had it sprayed immediately. But I found out later that these holes had been drilled—and for a purpose. During the Second World War, the desk had fallen into the hands of the Germans. They had heard the Russians had hidden a cachet of jewels in the desk, so they drilled it full of holes to try and discover any secret compartments. But they couldn't find any—and neither have I. I even had the desk X-rayed to make sure there were no hidden treasures, sometimes you can find interesting documents concealed in old furniture. Alas, nothing showed up. But you never know!

I first saw the desk in a privately owned museum in Pensacola, Florida. A woman by the name of Mrs. Wilson, who was then about 83 years old, had an amazing collection of all the treasures she had assembled in her lifetime. Eventually, she had decided to share her collection with the world and had made the greater part of her home a museum open to the public. The money she took from admission fees she donated to the church. She felt she was contributing pleasure, therefore, by sharing her treasure with the world.

When I came along, however, Mrs. Wilson had suffered several burglaries. And being an old lady living alone, she had begun to feel it was not worth getting hit over the head by some intruder merely for a few valuable possessions. She told me it had become a burden running her museum. So she offered me the entire contents for a very nominal sum—with the sole condition that I make a substantial donation to her favorite charity, which was, of course, the church. The desk was one of the items in her collection.

There were many other things, of course. The chandelier I have in my Palm Springs dining room came from that same museum. And a huge circular French tapestry, which was over twenty feet wide—it really belonged in a Palace. The tapestry was so huge, alas, that I could not find a place for it anywhere, and so had to sell it.

Much of the furniture and decoration in my Palm Springs house was relatively inexpensive compared with that desk, of course. But in other ways, The Cloisters has become a veritable Aladdin's cave; in fact, the house contains many of my favorite things. Not all of them are valuable in terms of money; but all of them are very special to me. Why don't we have a look around?

In my entry hall, I have a collection of icons from different parts of the world—many are from Greece. Most are hand painted, and some date back to the sixteenth and seventeenth centuries. Next to them I have a mirror which once belonged to the King of Spain and is over five hundred years old; it is hand carved out of wood and covered in gold leaf.

This is the dining room, with that chandelier I told you about. Originally, it was a gas chandelier. I had the whole thing electrified, but you can still adjust its height by means of a pulley system. You can lower the center part in order to fill the oil font, which is in the center.

The furniture is part of my Randolph Hearst collection. I call it such because of its similarity to what he collected at San Simeon. In fact, Hearst's eldest son came by one time and tried to sell me some of the original San Simeon furniture. But when he showed me pictures of it, I told him I had it already! The table seats fourteen comfortably, although there are eight more leaves I can put in to make it longer. Any way you look at it, it's huge.

The silver plateau down the middle of the table is from a mansion in Colorado Springs. It's made of mirrored sterling silver, and on it I place different trimmings for different times of the year. At Christmas, for example, I have it set up with the Nativity scene, and it's really beautiful.

I suppose my pride and joy in the dining room, however, is my Queen Elizabeth glassware. It is exactly like hers, except that instead of an E being engraved on each piece, there is an L—although I did manage to keep the same Royal crest and pattern which had been made for Queen Elizabeth. It was designed by the Moser Crystal Company in Czechoslovakia, which makes glass for Kings and Queens and the Pope and the Maharajahs. In recent years, they have expanded, to make glassware for celebrities; they engraved a set for Sophia Loren, for instance. And when I heard they had made glasses for Sophia Loren, I thought, well, they can make some for me. Normally they never use the same pattern for two different people. But, as I was about to give a Royal Command Performance in London, I thought it would be nice to have a pattern exactly like that of the Queen. I asked permission, and it was granted.

There are 376 pieces of glass altogether in the collection—everything from stemware to tumblers and aperitif glasses, from fingerbowls and fruit compotes to decanters, from pitchers to schnapps glasses. In fact, there is a glass for every kind of wine and for every kind of liqueur. They cost a fortune! The duty alone was $3,000, so the glasses must be worth somewhere around $42,000. Everybody says to me "Do you use them?" I most certainly do. In fact, I use them all the time, although afterwards they are always washed very carefully and by hand. They *never* go in the dishwasher. When I knew I had

finally bought them, I was so excited that I even had special cupboards designed with mirrors and shelves. I had no idea precisely what shapes the glasses were going to be, but I think it worked out rather well, don't you?

In all, I have twenty-five different place settings which can be used with these glasses. I have a service in gold and a service in sterling, so I can set a table all gold or set it all silver. The silver set I have collected from various parts of the world. Most of the filigree work is English; the candelabras are from Italy. I got those in duty free! After all, although they're new, they are still works of art.

Besides my Royal glasses, I have a considerable collection of other glassware. Much of it comes from Europe, except for certain red glasses which come from Disneyworld in Florida! In fact, red glass is very valuable now, and I do think it's pretty with all the lights shining through it. I also have some very early American handcut crystal, most of which is signed.

As you know, I believe it never hurts an antique to be used for something other than that for which it was intended. I had an old cupboard, for instance, which was going to ruin. So I took out its shelves and turned it into a television cabinet. It now sits in my dining room and I think is rather fine. I *like* things to be useful. I *use* my fine crystal; I use my silver. I would make a French commode into cabinets for my hi-fi speakers rather than throw away a rotting and otherwise useless commode. I would never destroy the original antique, however. If at any later time I wanted to transfer it back to its original state, I could.

Most of the glass in my bathroom is French Baccarat; the chandelier over the Jacuzzi bathtub is from a church. In the corner is a white marble carrara statue that came from Rome, and all the ceilings and walls are mirrors. At the side I have another of those French *armoires*; this one I have turned into a sink, with gold and onyx fixtures and a golden porcelain basin. I have even put a miniature chandelier in it!

On either side are two pedestals, which almost represented a total disaster. Originally, they were white porcelain. But as I had wanted something darker to match the *armoire*, I thought, "Oh well, I will finish them myself." I splattered them with walnut varnish, and then wiped away what I didn't want. Finally, I blended in the varnish with my fingers and the finished result was not too bad, except when I moved the pedestals to where they are now.

Above, the tower in my Palm Springs
house, one of the original parts of the
building I was able to save. And right,
my St. Anthony chapel. Once upon a
time, it was full of vending machines;
I'm sure you'll agree it has improved
since then. The stained glass window I
found in Providence, Rhode Island.

Left is my red glassware, which is beautiful with light shining through it, don't you think? Below is my silver service, which has been collected from all over the world. I also set my table gold.

My dining room, which seats fourteen, has been the scene of many rewarding dinner parties. The chandelier has been electrified, and gives the room a cheerful quality, don't you think?

Left is my Czar Nicholas II desk on which the Franco-Russian Alliance was signed. In World War II, the Germans riddled it full of holes to try and find hidden treasure. Alas, we're still looking! Below left is part of my main bathroom; the statue is of white Carrara marble, the crystal is French Baccarat. Right, my throne! And below, my Valentino room with its sleigh bed. The chandelier also came from his estate. The piano, inevitably, was mine!

The garden of my Palm Springs house, including that notorious fountain, top right. Above is the view from my sitting room. The local chamber of commerce tells me that the average temperature is in the high seventies and low eighties all year round. It's amazing, therefore, that we manage to keep the garden looking so fresh.

Above is a peep into the dining room, complete with its William Randolph Hearst furniture. You can just see the cabinet which houses my Czechoslovakian glassware.

Top left, two views of The Cloisters. And below left, my swimming pool.

Right is the master bedroom. Note the barrel roof, which I have had restored, and of course, the chandelier. When people ask me why I need twin beds, I tell them that one is for me, and the other for the dogs!

The Weston family chess set. I'm glad chess is such a peaceful game.

I discovered that I had left big squares of varnish stain on the carpet! I thought I'd ruined a priceless carpet. Luckily, I found a product that took the stain out. But it was a nasty moment.

Then there is my "throne"! Everybody gets a kick out of that! The idea was simple really. I hate toilets which look like toilets, so I made this one look like a throne!

Next we come to one of my more spectacular rooms, which is dominated by a bed that once belonged to Rudolph Valentino. (You will remember that my mother called me Valentino after the great movie star; and she called my brother Rudolph.) When I first discovered Valentino's bed, however, it was dismantled and in a very bad and tarnished condition, merely wrapped together with rope. I bought it, hoping to find that all the parts were there. In fact, some of the little pieces were missing, although (luckily) nothing of importance. So I had the whole thing dipped and cleaned and brought back to its original condition.

Curiously enough, it's a very long bed, although Rudolph Valentino was never considered tall. The chandelier also came from his estate. That too was all in bits and very black. But I put it together and polished it and rescued it. Much of the other furniture and decorations in this room are over a hundred years old and now only found in museums. The chess set, for example, was given to the granddaughter of the Weston family (the makers of Weston Guns) as a wedding gift in 1890. Altogether the room is exceptionally cosy and, on certain nights when I feel my master bedroom is a little too fancy, I'll sneak down to my Rudolph Valentino room and sleep there. Just for fun.

The garden, alas, is always a problem, especially in this hot climate. Palm Springs is very mild even when it is very cold, if you see what I mean. Most times of the year we never have temperatures below the high 70's or the low 80's, including the winter time. The Chamber of Commerce insists that the average temperature is 82 degrees. But the heat, or rather the lack of rain, makes it extremely difficult, for example, to grow grass. Of course, it's not as bad as Las Vegas, which is still hotter and in which, during the summer, it can get up to about 120 degrees. Sometimes, it's so hot there you could fry an egg on the sidewalk. In such heat it is almost impossible to achieve any reasonable landscaping, and, if you leave your lawn for a week without water, it will go brown. It will burn!

But even in Palm Springs I need a gardener 52 weeks of the year, just to keep everything fresh and green. There are many houses, of course, which cannot afford to keep a gardener. There are also certain department stores and banks, certain business buildings that close during the summer and so cannot tend their gardens properly. Consequently, an entire industry devoted to artificial landscaping—which does not require too much care and which can easily stand the heat of the summer—has arisen. One of their experts might suggest including a palm tree, for instance, to make the grass and the flowers appear more natural. But often the palm tree finishes up looking more fake than the rest.

My only concession to this make-believe gardening is in my choice of flowers. I admit that the flowers on my piano are usually made of silk. I used to have plastic flowers, but these I don't care for because after a while they develop a mildewed smell. They also get brittle and break. The only reason I went for them in the beginning was to get an instant look, and the quickest way to achieve that was to go artificial. But, in view of the shortage of good gardeners (as well as the considerations of climate), maybe this is the way all landscaping and gardening will develop in the future.

Anyway, as we discussed before, I have no real objection to the fake. I love my Palm Springs fireplace, partly because everybody thinks the logs are real, but they are not. The flames, for instance, are pure gas. Perhaps what makes the fire seem real, however, are the "ashes"—actually they're shredded asbestos. Asbestos doesn't burn. It gets red hot and looks like ash. It even goes white when it cools, just as ash does. When I discovered that you could buy fake ashes, I went out and bought several bags and put them all over all my fireplaces! After all, cleaning out a real fireplace often creates more and more dirt around the house.

Later I discovered you can even buy incense to put onto a gas log fire which makes it *smell* exactly like a real fire. You can get any kind of incense to match the wood that you wish to smell—mahogany, pine or oak. You put this substance on the gas logs and, every now and then, it will crackle and pop almost like a real fire. I have had people standing right next to it and saying, "Oooh, that *feels* so good," although actually it gives off little or no heat at all.

Incidentally, the iron grills and the iron urns that you see throughout the garden came from a cemetery in Austria. They used to hold flowers and plants, but here I used them in a somewhat happier way.

It seems, therefore, that I'm always finding things which are in need of tender loving care. My house in Palm Springs is only one example of a structure or an antique which I have been able to save. I admire beautiful things, obviously, but I admire even more seeing some ugly duckling things become beautiful. Sometimes it's very difficult to help people in such a direct way, most of them are very sensitive to change. But you can always help a piece of furniture. Once I found a beautiful chest which someone had painted white—yet another antique ruined with a lot of paint. I spent ages—and a small fortune—restoring it. I am sure if I had searched long enough I would have found a chest nearly as beautiful (and probably much cheaper) that was already finished. But it was much more fun bringing something back from the dead.

And, of course, your work of restoration is never finished. I love doing things around the house. I love building new fireplaces or refinishing old furniture. I love painting. There was a time when I used to spend a lot of time with oils and watercolors. Alas, every time I painted a piece of art I gave it away. I was pleased to have painted it, of course, although much more pleased when I gave it away. I wish I'd kept some of them now. I do have a few examples—I painted a couple of hunting dogs, for example, and entered them in an art competition in Wisconsin. Luckily, and much to my surprise, they won first prize.

I'm also constantly finding bric-a-brac, of which a part is broken, and so the entire object is reckoned useless. I have a bunch of things like that, which nobody wants. People say, "Oh, the stand is missing." So they throw away the whole contraption. I've got boxes and boxes of bits and pieces that cry out for a missing piece in order to make them whole again. Decanters with the stoppers missing, for example. Everywhere I go one of the first things I look for is a stopper for one of my decanters.

I just hate to see *anything* deteriorate, however inexpensive or trivial. I love wicker furniture, for instance. To me it represents an era—Scott Fitzgerald, the Great Gatsby and all of that. It's not an era I am altogether familiar with, but it was an important decade in American history. It had great style, and I hate to think of it being totally destroyed.

The Roxy Theatre in New York, which has been torn down now, was a great example of Art Deco. New York's Radio City Music Hall is on the verge of being demolished because it's no longer financially profitable to keep it open. Yet it too is another great example of that period, and if it goes, I can just see dealers from all over the world converging on it like locusts to buy up railings and carvings and whatever. The whole thing will be destroyed, and an era will be lost.

I suppose this concern for the past is one of the reasons why, in my houses, I love to create "eras." I have always been fascinated with the Victorian age, for example. So one room in my home in Hollywood is strictly Victorian. If I feel in a Victorian mood, I'll grab a book and go there to read about Queen Victoria. Then there is my Rudolph Valentino room in Palm Springs.

I furnish all my houses with this objective very much in mind. None have the same decor in each room. There's a little bit of this and a little bit of that. And I am often drawn to certain sections of my houses because they remind me of something in the past with which—for that moment—I wish to identify.

Even so, I don't really think there is any era I would rather have lived in than the present one—not least because of the tremendous opportunities that living today has afforded me. But wouldn't it be fascinating if we could transport ourselves into an era when people didn't pay any taxes! Just think of that!

Below, the cemetery gates I rescued from Austria.
Right, my breakfast arbor, complete with real grapes!

Marriage, Dogs, and Being Myself

I suppose that as long as I remain a bachelor people are going to ask me why I have never married. I don't think too many people know this, but I come from a family of divorce, which has made quite an imprint on my mind. The unity of marriage is for me a sacred thing—I don't believe in trial marriages. If I had got married, I would probably have been much like my brother George. When you have so much love to give, it is impossible for one person to receive it all. So you have to spread it around a little. And unless your wife is exceptionally understanding, she will get terribly jealous, and before you know it you have problems. Sometimes, you finish up with divorce—as in the case of my brother George. I can honestly say, however, that George is now happily married . . . for the fifth time.

I came very close to getting married two or three times, but some incident always occurred that gave me warning of what to expect. I would rather enjoy my freedom and enjoy my romances, without ensnaring myself in legal entanglements. And the longer I have my freedom, the more precious it seems to become.

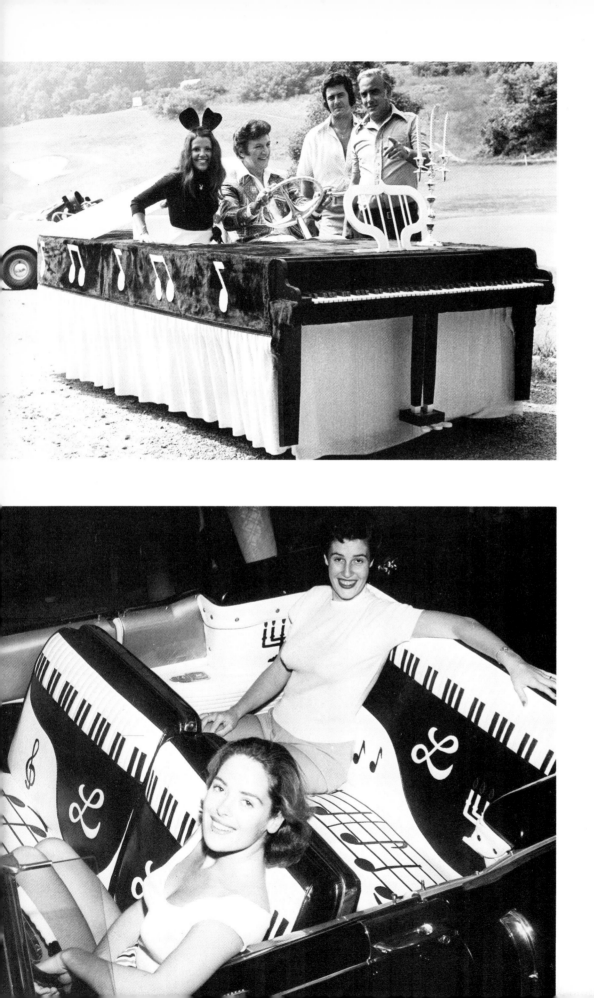

But, I think I would have loved to have had children. I admit that not being surrounded by children sometimes makes me feel quite lonely. I would have been a wonderful father. I wouldn't spoil my children, but I would share with them and give them all my love. I would hope to instill much of the proper knowledge and understanding that is needed to live in the world today. And I am quite sure that since I am able to do it with animals and cats and dogs and make *them* respond to love and affection, I would be all right with children.

Anyway, I wish I could adopt children like I adopt dogs. The reason I have so many dogs—I have fourteen altogether—is because the majority are animals that no one else wanted. I once made the horrible discovery that unwanted dogs have short lives; if nobody claims them or picks them up at the Humane Society or wherever, they are destroyed. So when somebody says, "I'm going to give this dog to the Humane Society," I usually adopt it myself, because in my experience the Humane Society is not so humane.

The dogs are now very much a part of my family. I call them children, and they answer to their names. When it's time for them to go for a ride or to go to bed or to go outside, I say, "Come on, children," and they come to attention.

They all get along very well together, although they are many different breeds, all with their individual personalities. I had one dog who was almost totally blind; I had to carry him around because he kept bumping into things. I was his eyes; I used to show him where

the doors were and where the chairs were that he could jump on. He could see faintly, but he couldn't distinguish. One day, I discovered there were actually three doctors in the country who performed operations on dogs' eyes. So I took him to the one that was nearest to Los Angeles. At first, the surgeon refused to operate until the dog had sufficient strength in his blood vessels to perform this delicate operation. During four months I gave the dog all the eye drops the doctor had given me, until eventually the blood vessels were strong enough for the operation to be carried out. Luckily, the operation was a success, and the dog can now see again. He's always been my most favorite dog, because he needed me the most.

Another of my little dogs—whose name was Seymour, after my manager—drowned in my fountain at Palm Springs. He was trying to retrieve a toy that had fallen into the pond and got sucked down by the pressure of the water. That night, I was distraught. I told everybody I never wanted to see the fountain work again. I felt strongly that this dog had been wasted, because of a ridiculous fountain. But instead of carrying out my wishes, my couple in Palm Springs—Madeleine and Gregory—had the fountain redesigned so that the dogs had steps to walk down into the fountain without falling in. And now the dogs have all had swimming lessons, so—reluctantly—I've started the fountain. It cost about $1300, to put steps in the fountain, but it was worth it. I would feel terrible if anything happened to one of the other dogs.

As I said, most of the dogs were given to me by people who didn't want them. I have a Shetland sheepdog that had been kept in a cage for six months. I felt that this dog should have its freedom. It wasn't that easy, however, because when I got the dog home and out of his cage, he was like a frightened animal that had been kept in captivity too long. He ran around like a wild animal and had no control of his nerves or his nervous system. It was extremely difficult to break him of the memory of having been caged for six months. But now he has become very gentle and friendly. It takes time and patience, but the sheepdog is great company and I love him.

If I'm alone in Palm Springs, although I have had the table set just for me, I always have eight or ten little heads sitting on the other chairs and waiting for some morsel I might leave over at the end of the meal. When you are that close to your dogs, moreover, after a while you get to talk to them like people. And because Madeleine and Gregory speak French and Rumanian, all the dogs speak three lan-

guages! I think they're smarter than I am, because I can only speak one language.

Then, there is Jacques. My heart went out to him because he was one of the scrawniest dogs I had ever seen. But now he is turning out to be one of the pretty ones!

Mishi was owned by a very nice young lady and refused to stay home alone when the young lady went to work. But, because she couldn't take him to work with her, she gave him to me.

Now, for Bonaparte. The people who had Bonaparte moved back East and were not allowed to have a dog in their new apartment. And so Bonaparte came to live with us.

Lisa was sent to me all the way from Brisbane, Australia. She is two years old now.

As for Prego—he is a German Schnauzer with an Italian name which means "You're welcome."

My dogs make me feel very wanted. These apart, however, I can honestly say that I have never lacked friends. Nor have I ever felt rejected. Most of the people who surround me are not Johnny-Come-Latelys. They're people who have been with me for twenty years, and I like to think they'll be loyal and faithful for the rest of my life— not because I have *enriched* their lives, but because they have enriched mine. Nothing is really pleasurable when you try to enjoy it by yourself. It's only when you see or hear or touch or feel something in the presence of others that it becomes memorable.

Even so, I don't think any one individual could supply the love I get from my audience, or even the love I get from my work. If ever I did meet a person with whom I wanted to live, that person would have to understand that my love has to be shared—that it belongs not just to an individual, but to many people. Once, for example, back in the late fifties, I had planned a beach party with a particular lady to which we had invited all our friends. But two days before the beach party, I got a call inviting me to take part in a concert at the Hollywood Bowl. Up until that time, I had never played at the Hollywood Bowl, although it had obviously been one of my dreams, one of my ambitions. I was so excited and thrilled about being invited that I called her up and said, "Guess what, I have been invited to play the Hollywood Bowl at last!" But her only reaction was, "What about our beach party?"

To me the beach party was *so* insignificant. You can go to a beach party any time, but you cannot play in the Hollywood Bowl at any time! I tried to explain this to her, but we had a furious argument. And the more I thought about it, the more despondent I became. So my career is my first love. My public and my work, these are my first concerns.

I also love my fellow performers and care very much that new talent, especially if it's young, should have a proper chance to show its mettle. I have always tried, therefore, to introduce new acts during

One of my protégés, the banjo player Scotty Plummer. It gives me such pleasure to introduce new talent and then watch them go on to become stars.

190

my show, although it now takes a lot of money to get someone launched in a career. There are coaching and lessons. All this has to be planned, arrangements have to be made, musicians have to be hired, and studios rented. Mostly these newcomers don't have a penny to begin with. So I have to furnish them with all the necessary back-

Another protégée.

ing. I have to costume them—once I even had to buy a girl's unmentionables. But I much prefer having these youngsters than a big name on my show. If I can provide an opportunity for a new star to emerge, like I did when I introduced Barbra Streisand in Las Vegas, then I feel part of my good fortune is being repaid.

Backstage, with two old friends and admirers.
Above, the irrepressible Jimmy Durante; and
right, the uniquely gifted Sammy Davis Jr.

With this in mind, I try to go around and visit all the other entertainers in whichever town I'm playing, especially Las Vegas. I find that my being there seems to give them a lift. Also, I try never to say anything bad about them. If I'm nuts about their performance and I really adore them, I go overboard and tell everybody about their particular act. But if I thought they were not at their best, I try to encourage them. I find that every one of those people I have been to visit come back to see me perform. And that is very flattering.

Three great stars I have had the honour of working with; above, the one and only Bob Hope; above right, the British comedian, Terry-Thomas; and below right, the late and much loved Jack Benny—and he never offered to pay me for accompanying him at the piano!

Tom Jones' birthday party. Left to right, Joan Rivers, Joey Heatherton, Sonny Bono, Tom, Dionne Warwicke, Debbie Reynolds and me. And what a noise we were making. You can tell from Tom's expression!

It seems to me, therefore, that the essence of all living things—whether they be dogs or human beings or fellow performers—is the feeling of being wanted, of knowing that somebody cares. And I do care. That's what life's all about. When my mother reckons she can oblige me with a favor or do me some good, she is only too anxious to help. She is never in my way, but always there when I need her. I truly love her for that.

I admit that I am intrigued by the tremendous urge, if that is the right word, to be loved. And I think, in order to satisfy that urge, I love tremendously in return. I love everybody; and, in return, I hope that some of my audience will love and care about me. Occasionally, however, that caring takes the most peculiar forms. Sometimes friends come down to my dressing room after a show and ask to use the washroom. Often they have to walk through where I have my costumes hanging and, would you believe, I have no end of small items lifted. I don't think anyone really means to steal; it's just that they want a souvenir. People even take crystals out of my chandeliers at home or fancy knobs from the bathroom doors. But some of my jeweled ties are worth $500 a piece, so the cost can be quite serious. I try to discourage people from taking my clothes, therefore, by having other things for them to take, like ashtrays or records or books. Those things can be easily replaced. The most valuable thing I have ever lost was a candelabra off the bonnet of my car. It had real diamonds in it. The chauffeur had gone for a coffee and a sandwich and when he came out, the candelabra was gone—literally torn out.

I admit I've been comparatively lucky. I think it's the way you approach a crowd. If you are open and extend your hand in a friendly handshake, people respond. I have always tried to avoid having a bodyguard, therefore, especially one that is armed. It tends to create mass hysteria. Anyway, I think my audience would resent the idea of bodyguards—negative people create negative things. If you surround yourself with negative people, it's *impossible* to have any positive thoughts.

Right, with Elton John, in Australia.
Below, receiving my Entertainer of the Year award,
in September, 1973. With me are Andy Griffith,
Don Rickles, and Peter Marshall.

If you didn't see the show, I don't think you would ever guess who is singing with me at the piano. Would you believe, it was Cher! And here we are rehearsing in my Hollywood house for her show. She's dressed as "Laverne," and it was quite an experience.

I hope I've maintained a certain humanism about myself. I know I'm a star, but I do not believe in false modesty. And anyway, being a star doesn't always guarantee you special treatment. Once, I was staying at the Waldorf Hotel in New York and had gone down early before my evening performance. I was getting ready to do a series of one nighters, which is probably the most taxing thing an entertainer can do, but also one of the most profitable. I was wearing a rather smart suit and had a scarf around my neck. The maître d'hôtel came up to me and said he was very sorry but he could not let me into the restaurant without a tie. Well, I said, surely a scarf is a tie. And he said, "No, it isn't." So I went out to the hallway, took off the scarf, made it into a tie and walked in again. This time the guy said nothing. He just looked daggers at me. So you see, I get the same problems that everyone else does.

Trying to be positive, of course, can sometimes lead to problems. I know, for example, that many people think I smile too much, that I come across too damn pleasant or whatever. But I find that people are often taken aback in my presence because the man in person is so different from what most people expect. I believe this is because I reflect a lot of problems which exist in all Americans. We are very insecure in ourselves and in our culture. Everyone feels they *ought* to be doing what they want to do, and doing it the way they want to do it. But most people are too frightened to allow themselves that opportunity. So it's probably quite unnerving to meet someone like me who has the guts to be himself.

Anyway, I never worry about my critics. I know every joke that has ever been told about me. And now I have learned how to kid myself. When I started to do *that*, moreover, the critics had no room left to move—because how can you kid a kid?

My Image and the Press

A full evening at the theatre must contain elements that make you laugh, that make you cry, that make you angry, that make you sad, and that shock you. I am sure a little shock value in a performance is most important. *All* of these things are necessary, I believe, for a complete performance. When I go to see a show myself, I don't want to walk away at the end feeling hungry. I want to be fulfilled.

I was giving a concert one time in Florida, when all the lights went out—a total blackout. There's nothing darker than a darkened auditorium—when even the exit lights have gone out—and it could have been a very panicky situation. But I asked myself what would have happened back in the time of Chopin or Bach? They didn't have electric lights; they didn't have microphones. And yet they had some of the world's greatest artists and composers. So I made an announcement to the audience, "Let's pretend we're back in the time of Chopin," I said, "when there was no electric light." Suddenly, candles appeared and I gave a real candlelight performance. Amazingly, everybody stayed. No one missed the air-conditioning or the amplified sound, and the concert became an historical performance in modern day times. I often wonder what would happen to many of the rock 'n' roll groups if somebody pulled *their* plug. They'd be out of business.

This kind of initiative I am sure I learned from my great hero, Al Jolson. He also made his audience feel they were getting something more than they had paid for. At the end of his show, he would come down a ramp and sing four or five additional songs. He did this every night, of course, but the audience thought they were getting the extra just for them. Something extra, that was his motto.

THE MILWAUKEE JOURN

Wladzin Valentino Liberace Coming

With Mom in London, 1969. I think she enjoyed it more than I did. She always likes to travel, so she tells me!

Another inspiration was Lily Pons, and from her, too, I learned a considerable lesson. She was the only singer at the Metropolitan Opera who had written into her contract that she would always have a spotlight follow her on stage wherever she went so that she stood out like a jewel. She was a tiny person and, in a massive opera production, it was easy enough for her to get lost. So Miss Pons always wore light colors—pinks and whites and pastels—in order to be seen. When I started playing in big stadiums, therefore, I too wore light colors and stayed away from blacks or browns. This sense of stagecraft, and of knowing your proper place on that stage, I grasped from watching Al Jolson and Lily Pons. They were experts at it, and I felt I owed it to myself to learn from them and learn well.

Of course, *most* stagecraft is full of trickery or little deceits. And the essence of a successful show is surprise. I love to introduce this element into my shows, although sometimes it isn't quite the surprise I had planned. When I was doing my television series in London, for example, the writers of the show came up with what they called a gimmick. Knowing I am fond of my mother and that I speak of her so often, they thought it would be a great idea to fake a telephone call from her in California. The idea seemed interesting enough, but when they produced the script for the telephone conversation, it was not my mother at all. They had made her out to be a real showbiz mother, which she is not. She is a very simple, direct and sincere person. She speaks her mind and says what she truly feels. But she is never a contrived personality. So I said, "Well, if you really want to do this and make it believable, why don't you put a real call through to my mother during the show? You can amplify her voice so that the audience can hear the conversation." They thought this was a great idea.

Having sold them on the idea, however, I suddenly began to have second thoughts. Knowing that my mother is apt to say almost about *anything*, I was tempted to warn her. But, after worrying about it a great deal, I decided eventually to leave it all to fate.

So, in the middle of my television show, with some four hundred people in the studio and countless thousands watching at home, the call came from mother in Hollywood. She still didn't know that I was in a television studio, but imagined, I suppose, that I was calling from my hotel room. We exchanged pleasantries like, "Hello, how are you?" and that sort of thing. But then her first remark (which got

quite a laugh) was, "Why don't you write me a letter instead of spending all this money on a telephone call?" So I said, "Well, Ma, there's nothing like hearing your voice on the phone and talking to you in person." I went on, "How are you, by the way? You haven't really told me how you are feeling." And she said, "Well, I'm not feeling too good. I have a little arthritis in my legs . . ." and then she started complaining! Oh, how she complained! So I said, "Well that's too bad, Ma, because I am talking to you from the studio in the middle of my London television show, and I was hoping you might feel well enough to come over to London in person and make an appearance on my television show! Just a minute," I said. "Hold on while I ask the audience in the studio if they would like you to come to London." And they screamed and yelled their approval, so I said, "Did you hear that Ma?" And she said, "Fine, I love it! When?" "But wait a moment," I said. "You have just been telling me about all your arthritis and your other aches and pains!" "Nonsense," she said. "I never felt better in my life!" And that got a huge laugh!

My career has not always been as successful as it is now, unfortunately. The fifties and early sixties were very good to me. But during the middle sixties, I got stuck somehow in the doldrums. Absolutely nothing seemed to go right. I am the last person to blame others for my misfortunes but, looking back, I am sure many of my problems were created by the Press. I think they took advantage of my mother, for example. My relationship with my mother was no more and no less than anybody else's. I liked her, so I took care of her. But I took care of all my family, including my surviving brother and my sister. The publicity men and the Press used my love for my mother, however, because it gained audience ratings for my television show and readers for their columns. The mothers all said, "Wow. Doesn't he treat his mother nice! He *must* be a good boy." Also, being the first matinee idol of television, I found that even my curly hair was used by the promotion people. I began to feel I had been totally *designed* by the Press. All that nonsense is hard for me to remember clearly because now I am as much a comic and an entertainer as I am a mother-loving pianist. But the notion that loving my mother was my only talent still hurts.

In fact, I am very sensitive to criticism. And I always listen to it. I remember one writer in Toronto—she was a young lady, I think—attacking me because we were a few minutes late for her interview. Alas, our flight had been delayed so we were really not to blame. But

I knew immediately when I saw her that she was going to get me because she was so mad about having been kept waiting. Later, during the interval of my show, in an attempt to forestall her, I announced that there was a certain writer in Toronto who made it her business to write unflattering stories as a way of filling up the theater! The audience laughed, but I was not too sure about the young lady. Nowadays, when someone says something particularly cruel, I offer them my autobiography and say, "Read this, and maybe afterwards you will know me a little bit better."

That Toronto journalist was particularly unfair because usually I like to give my undivided attention to whomever is interviewing me. I try to answer all their questions and listen as much as I talk. And I never mind if journalists finish up not liking me, provided they have got to know me a little first. After all, the thing that makes me look forward to each performance is the fact that I know there are people in my audience who couldn't care less about me. I concentrate on winning them over, therefore, and the greatest satisfaction I can have out of a performance is to know I have made converts. I am sure I would have been discouraged a long time ago if I knew I had to face an audience of worshippers every night.

So I like to think that if I am able to meet with another person, either in performance or through personal contact, then I can say or do something that might at least make them consider changing their attitude toward me. Most of my dissenters or those who don't dig me are people who really don't know me. My task, therefore, is to get better acquainted!

At my Cassandra trial, for instance, it came out that the man had never been exposed to me, except for a brief moment on television. He had never met me personally, and yet had formed this very complete opinion about me. I felt this was unfair and I was hurt. It would have been marvellous, however—even after he had written about me —if I could have met him and talked it out and not had to go through the court. I would much rather have said, "Come over and let's meet. I consider what you have written to be untrue, so perhaps you will allow me the opportunity to present my side. Perhaps you will afford me the same amount of column inches to write a reply." Alas, this proved to be impossible.

I had a similar experience with a columnist in San Francisco. At a press conference I attended I was introduced to everyone in the usual way—I went round shaking hands and meeting everyone. There

was one man whose name did not immediately register, but whom I found most charming. I thought he was particularly intelligent and most witty. Eventually, he said to me, "I can't understand why you are being so nice to me! I have never said a good thing about you in my columns and I would have thought you had abundant reason to dislike me." And then, of course, I remembered who he was. I suppose if I had been tipped off that he was the San Francisco journalist who had written more terrible columns about me than the whole of the West Coast press put together, I might have avoided him. But not realizing who he was, I had started chatting with him. And now he admitted that, having met me, he couldn't honestly say he disliked me. He said he really hoped we would become friends.

As I've said before, nobody kids myself more than I do. I think the public appreciates the fact that I get an even bigger charge out of my costumes, my candelabra and all my showmanship than even they do. The only thing I resent, therefore, is when the criticism goes below the belt. I find there is a sort of cancerous journalism which sets out to destroy a person, and this is very difficult to correct. The fact was that a total stranger, like Cassandra, had said something both distasteful and damaging. People, who had never been aware of my presence, at reading what he had written might instantaneously hate me. That was unforgivable.

I believe in freedom of speech, obviously. This is one of the great freedoms of the world. But sometimes, certain people hide behind this cloak and use it in a way that attempts to humiliate others. Most citizens, and particularly most entertainers, are not able to fight back as I was. Normally, everyone says, "Oh well, this is all part of show business," and shrug their shoulders and live with it. But I was unable to live with it. I had become the butt of too many unpleasant jokes. My character had been assassinated—not my shownmanship, not my piano playing, not my costumes or my candelabra, but me as a person. This I could not endure. I fought and, I am happy to say, I won. And, in the case of my London libel suit, I didn't do it for the money. In fact, I donated all the money awarded me to charity. But I won what was for me an important battle.

"How Lucky Can You Get?"

Several years ago, as I was starting out on my career, a famous numerologist did a chart of my life. When it was completed, I read it over. But it was so fantastic—the things he reckoned would happen to me—that I tossed it aside as the musings of a maniac who was, after all, just a fortune teller. He predicted I would be the subject of a scandalous trial, that I would live in splendor, and that I would have many beautiful homes. He also said I had been born under a set of signs and symbols that gave me an almost magical kind of endurance. He cited an example which I still recall. He said, "Even if you were facing a firing squad, before they counted to ten, someone would step in to save you."

Once, as you know, I had the last rites. I actually planned my funeral as long ago as 1963. I've updated the details since then; instead of a burning flame outside my coffin, I now want a burning candelabra. Anyway, I always thought that if someone told me I was going to die, I would become very emotional. But, to my surprise, although I felt sad, I was confident I had lived a full and wonderful life. I had done many things in my lifetime that other people had not done. So I decided that, if this was the way it was going to be, I would put my store in order and make out my will. And when that was done, I asked my business manager if I had any money left, because I said I would like the pleasure of spending it—not on myself, because I was a lost cause, but on other people. He told me that, in cold hard cash, after taking care of everybody, I had about three-quarters of a million dollars left.

So I proceeded to spend three-quarters of a million dollars. I bought presents that you wouldn't believe. I would look through magazines during the night, and then next day would get on the phone and start opening accounts. I bought things for people that I

felt they should have but had never been able to afford. I bought my
mother the most expensive mink coat in her life! I also bought her
some beautiful real jewelry from Tiffanys—diamonds, rubies, emer-
alds and pearls. I bought motorcycles and automobiles. I even bought
a house for somebody. It took me about two weeks to spend the
money until, finally, I was broke.

Next, I decided to organize a Christmas party at my home in
Hollywood that no one who came would ever be likely to forget. I
wanted everyone to receive their gifts at the party. Sadly, I would not
be there to enjoy their happiness because the doctors had told me it
was very unlikely I would ever see another Christmas. So it was important to decorate my home in the most fantastic way. I called a very
dear friend who had worked with me for nearly twenty years and
said, "How would you like to decorate my home for Christmas?" (I
never told him that I didn't expect to be there.) I said that because
I was coming home for Christmas, I wanted it to be super fabulous.
So he said, "How much can I spend?" And I said, "Well, will $25,000
be enough?" He just fell on the floor. Eventually, he picked himself
up and said, "You obviously want the most beautiful Christmas
decorations that money can buy." And I said, "Yes, I do."

As luck would have it, however, something miraculous happened.
If ever I discovered I had faith, I discovered it then. A little Sister

Christmas is a very special occasion for me; indeed, I seem to spend the entire year preparing. Fancy dress is not optional at my parties! I once spent $25,000 just decorating the house, although admittedly that was rather extraordinary, even for me.

came into my hospital room and said, "Everybody in this hospital is praying for you. But," she added, "sometimes it takes your own prayers as well." Then she handed me a little book called *Saint Anthony's Treasury*. (Saint Anthony was the saint who was considered the doctor of the Church and the worker of miracles). She had designated certain prayers in this book that she thought I should recite. So I prayed to Saint Anthony and, to make a long story short, I left the hospital on December 22nd and was home for Christmas!

Religion is something very personal for me. I think it comes from within. I *am* a religious man in the sense I believe there is a greater power than us. My experience in the hospital, moreover, taught me also that there is great power in faith. And I am sure that what you truly believe, and the way you live and the way you treat other people, is religion. It's not keeping to a schedule or going to church when you are supposed to go. I attend Church when the spirit moves me. Often, I find great contentment going into an empty church and spending a few moments in quiet contemplation. I am perhaps more religious than many people who go to church by the clock or the calendar. For me, all religions are wonderful because they all preach good. They all teach love for your fellow man. I was brought up as a Roman Catholic, but I am sure that had I been brought up as a Jew or an Episcopalian or a Lutheran or even an Evangelist I would have been no different from what I am now.

And Christmas, I guess, *is* the most looked-forward-to day of my life. The Christmas ornaments and that whole magical element of Christmas is a very special occasion for me. I possess a manger scene, for example, that I picked up in Houston, Texas. It is handmade, including the animals. In fact, the skin of the animals is actually real skin. The whole thing is unbelievably beautiful.

There is absolutely no end to what I will organize for celebrating Christmas. One year, my wardrobe manager Bob Fisher covered the ceiling of my Hollywood home with twinkling lights so that they looked like stars. Then I put a Christmas tree on a dais in the center of the living room, which appeared to go through the stars into the ceiling. It cost thousands of dollars because later on we had to re-do the ceiling! Anyway, to cap it all I appeared at the celebrations in an gold lamé Santa Claus costume.

Another Christmas, I rented a motel—a very chic place—and put Christmas trees in every guest room as well as a complete bar. The invitations alone cost around $3,000.

I suppose, because of my generosity, some people think I'm a

dummy about money. But I'm not. I know when people are cheating me or using me. Frequently, however, people go to extraordinary lengths to deceive me. Once, when I was in New York, there was a couple who, I admit, were very cute and wanted me to get them into show business. They said they had a comedy act. They used to bring me presents and flowers every night, and they would always pick up the check at dinner. I kept thinking to myself, well they have to be up to something! But they never asked for anything. Nothing at all.

The night before I was due to close came the pitch. The couple wanted me to put up money for their act. They had prepared lengthy papers which explained why I had to give them $20,000, whereupon I would own a percentage of their act. I thanked them and asked my business manager to look into it out of courtesy; which was lucky, because he found out that this couple had gone around and worked this same routine a dozen times. They had sold percentages of their act to thirty or forty different companies and were already being looked for by the police. In fact, there *was* no act and they had no plans for any. What some people will do to set up a deal!

And speaking of money, not many people realize that I have a partner. Whenever I make a dollar, fifty cents of it goes to taxes. There was a time when if you made a million dollars, you had *made* a million dollars. You didn't have to say, "Well, only half of it belongs to me; the other half belongs to Uncle Sam." At the turn of the century, there really were no taxes of any consequence. Most of the early Newport mansions are from that era. When taxes came along, however, people suddenly discovered they could not afford to keep up those tremendous mansions with seventy or eighty rooms. So the houses were sold or divided up or often merely abandoned. Their loss has been incalculable. How America is changing!

The other thing that has changed the American way of life, of course, is the unions. Labor used to be a cheap commodity. Most of the people who were in labor had come over from Europe and were happy to work for their room and board and very little cash. Later, they became organized and powerful and created the unions. The cost of having servants became prohibitive—which was another reason why the wealthy moved from their big houses into their smaller houses. Although you could buy the old mansions quite cheaply, no one wanted them because they cost so much to maintain. Unless they were turned into historical monuments, open to the public, they just fell into disrepair and finally were pulled down.

I'm not saying that these homes should have been preserved as

bastions of the rich to the exclusion of all others. I know that if I lived in a palace all by myself I would be very lonely. I would also be very bored. I love people to share my homes with me. People have a way of making you feel they're responsible for it anyway. I often say, "I'm so glad you like it, because, after all, you bought it!" And sometimes they don't think I'm joking.

I have been poor. I have never been hungry, but I was certainly poor. Being brought up during the Depression was never easy. But somehow, thanks to the imagination of both my mother and father, we always managed to make ends meet. Our clothing may have had patches on it, but it was spotlessly clean. Today, I still don't feel particularly wealthy, and I still adore simple pleasures. What excites me most about my way of life today is being able to enjoy some of the things that my work has inevitably taken me away from—a stroll through the woods, for example, or a tour of a new shopping center, or a walk down a busy city street simply window shopping. When I relax, I love eating popcorn or watching television or entertaining my friends in my home, rather than a glamorous restaurant. In fact, I hardly ever go out when I am off the road. I would rather show films or play the piano, if that is what my friends want.

And, in spite of all my collections, I have never fallen in love with

I love Christmas carols; but then, who doesn't? This local boys' choir gave me a particular thrill one year.

JOHANNESBURG, SOUTH AFRICA

material objects. Truly. I like to enjoy them, and I like to take care of them, and hopefully leave them in better shape than when I bought them. But I am not in love with them. I don't cry over a broken glass or a broken plate. When something gets broken, I just say, "Well the stores are full!" And it's true. Material things are easy to acquire. But when you are dealing with human beings, that's another matter. You must not break or destroy them. You caress them; you fondle them; you love them.

In fact, I think I'm a very appreciative person. I really enjoy the gifts I am sent, for example. One time I received a hand-crocheted bedspread made out of gold thread. The thread alone must have been worth $700. Most people I know would have folded it up and put it to one side. But, even though there was no bed I could use it for, I would never throw anything like that away. So I cut it up and made it into a tablecloth for the main dining room. And it's gorgeous! Everybody is eating off a bedspread, whether they realize it or not.

An entertainer's function is to entertain, not to preach. So I'm very apolitical; I do not want to get involved in politics at all. An entertainer should stay out of it. Even so, I would like to feel that my presence on earth is going to be felt for a long time after I am gone. In order to make one's presence felt, however, one has to achieve certain things. At the moment I am trying to bring happiness through my work. That is one thing, certainly. But only a small part of it. Above all, I would like to feel that all the antiques I have collected, and all the houses I have restored and reconstructed, will be enjoyed by people for many years to come. This is why I work, and that is why I have put this book together, to share with you some of my good fortune and some of my beautiful possessions. I did not spend my years collecting in order to establish a private and secretive museum. What I have done, I hope, is provide pleasure and to save that which might otherwise have been destroyed.

Which brings us back where we began. I have to admit that whether you agree with my taste does not seriously affect me. I have always wanted to create an environment for myself within which I could entertain and be entertained. Often, for example, in Las Vegas, I used to take out various friends gambling. I would give each one $100 and say "Play for me. If you win, I'll share the winnings; if you lose, you owe me nothing." One night, there were fifteen of us. We all went broke except my chauffeur, Vince Cardell, who spent his last few dollars on the Keno game. He played the license number of my limousine; all the numbers came in, and he won $25,000! How lucky can you get?

Just a few of my many hundreds of Christmas cards. It's nice to have friends, don't you think?

CLARENCE HOUSE
S.W. 1

11th January, 1973

Dear Mr. Liberace,

Queen Elizabeth The Queen Mother bids me write and thank you very much for the record which you have sent.

Your kind thought of Her Majesty at Christmas time and your gift are much appreciated.

The Queen Mother asks me to send you her best wishes for 1973.

Yours sincerely,

Ruth Fermoy

Lady-in-Waiting

Mr. Liberace.

DDE

GETTYSBURG
PENNSYLVANIA 17325

Palm Desert, California
December 23, 1964

Dear Mr. Liberace:

I appreciate your kindness in sending the personalized desk set.

It was thoughtful of you to remember me, and Mrs. Eisenhower joins in extending best wishes for a happy Holiday Season.

Sincerely,

Dwight D. Eisenhower

Mr. Lee Liberace
Suite 607 Taft Building
1680 North Vine Street
Hollywood 28, California

Thank you for your holiday greeting

and best wishes for happiness

in the New Year

Lyndon B. Johnson *Lady Bird Johnson*

Epilogue

I can't believe how many wonderful events and changes have taken place since this book was first created and planned and went to press. Besides my Hollywood and Palm Springs homes, my permanent residences (homes 3, 4, and 5) are now in Las Vegas. My summer residences (homes 6 and 7) are at Lake Arrowhead and Malibu Beach. I have a Bicentennial red, white, and blue Rolls Royce Convertible. I've acquired six more assorted dogs, a black cat named Samantha (which is now named Sam because we discovered it's a boy) and I'm planning a new television series. I've been invited to Poland, Japan, and Russia. I've just signed a new two million dollar contract with the Hilton Hotel in Las Vegas . . . And as a matter of course I went through a complete physical at the Las Vegas Clinic and my good friend Dr. Elias Ghanem says I'm going to live to be a hundred. It looks like I'm going to have a lot to show you and talk about in my next book. Get ready for Liberace, Part Two!

ACKNOWLEDGMENTS

The author would like to thank the following photographers, who contributed most of the photographs in this book: Tommy Mitchell, Rob Maher, Jamie James, John Wykoff, John Hamilton, Robert Scott Hooper, Rob Plunkett, R.S.

The artwork that appears on p. 93 is by Rick Fox, and by Ed Sotto on p. 145.

The author would also like to thank the following sources for the remaining photographs: John Ascuaga's Nugget, p. 115; A.T.V. Network Ltd., p. 193; Austarama Television Pty. Ltd., p. 197; Chicago Photographers, p. 138; Furman Studio, p. 71; Dezzo Hoffmann, p. 146; Las Vegas News Bureau, p. 195; Earl Leaf, p. 181; Hayward Magie, p. 138; Doug McKenzie, p. 144; Don Meller, p. 183; Milwaukee Journal, p. 143; Mirror Newspapers, p. 211; Elliot Robinson, p. 148; Bill Watson, p. 197.

Special thanks to Mr. Tony Palmer, Mr. Seymour Heller, and Mr. Jamie James for their kind assistance in putting together this book.

This book was designed by
Libra Graphics, Inc.
101 Park Avenue, New York, N.Y. 10017